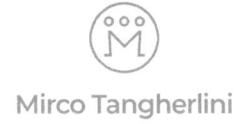

Mirco Tangherlini

The Art of Generating Personalized Styles with AI

ALCHEMY OF SREF CODES

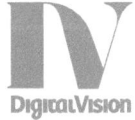

DigitalVision

Title
ALCHEMY OF SREF CODES - The Art of Generating Personalized Styles with AI

© **Digital Vision** Independent Editions

First Edition
Jule 2024

illustration of **Mirco Tangherlini**

tangherlini.it
ai-telier.it

If you are reading this brief essay on the "sref" function of MidJourney (MJ), it means you are already immersed in the fascinating universe of an extraordinary generative Artificial Intelligence platform.

Questo nuovo strumento rappresenta una vera e propria rivoluzione nel modo in cui creiamo e interagiamo con le immagini digitali.

This new tool represents a true revolution in how we create and interact with digital images.

MJ is much more than an image generation software; it is a gateway to a world of infinite creative possibilities, where technology and art harmoniously blend together. Artists can now explore new dimensions of their creativity, experimenting with styles and techniques they could only imagine before. The platform allows ideas to transform into visual reality with an ease and precision that seems almost magical.

The Artificial Intelligence at the core of MidJourney was developed with the intent to support and amplify artists' creative abilities, not to replace them. Each image generated with MJ is the result of a collaboration between human intuition and computational power, tirelessly working to realize the user's artistic vision. This synergy between man and machine opens new horizons in artistic production, enabling the creation of works that reflect unique depth and complexity.

Moreover, MidJourney is an inclusive platform, welcoming creatives of all experience levels. Whether you are an established artist seeking new tools to enrich your repertoire, or a beginner eager to explore the world of digital art, MJ offers an environment rich in resources and inspiration.

The "sref" function in particular, with its ability to apply unique and consistent styles to images, represents one of the most powerful and versatile aspects of this platform. Through MidJourney, technology becomes an extension of artistic thought, allowing traditional boundaries of visual creation to be surpassed.

Each image generated is a step forward in innovation, a testament to the infinite potential that can be achieved when art and science are united. MJ is a catalyst for your imagination, capable of taking you to places you never thought possible.

By using MidJourney, you become part of a pioneering community that is redefining the concept of art in the 21st century.

Questa piattaforma ti offre infatti gli strumenti per esplorare, sperimentare e innovare, trasformando ogni tua idea in una creazione visiva straordinaria ed è una porta aperta su un universo di possibilità creative senza confini.

You have surely already taken the first important step: you have registered with MidJourney and begun to explore its potential.

This means you already have a basic understanding of the functionalities offered by this platform and know how to use prompts to generate images. You have experimented with various available styles and started to grasp the immense possibilities that MidJourney offers to creatives worldwide.

However, beyond knowing the basic functionalities, you have likely heard of the "sref" function and become curious about how it can further enhance your creative process. "Sref," or style reference, is one of the most powerful and versatile tools offered by MidJourney, allowing you to apply unique and consistent styles to your creations.

This brief essay will guide you through the wonders of this function and show you how you can transform your ideas into breathtaking visual realities. Personally, I use MJ both commercially, as an editorial illustrator, and artistically, having several exhibitions of AI-generated works and an e-commerce site (**ai-telier.it**) that sells AI-created art.

What fascinates me the most is the "artistic" use of artificial intelligence, the possibility of creating true works of art. I am well aware that there is an ongoing debate between detractors who do not consider this tool a true generator of

art and those who, instead, fight to affirm that this new technology represents an additional opportunity for artists. This debate, passionate and intense, reflects the complexity and depth of contemporary perceptions of art and creativity. However, I prefer not to dwell on these polemics.

Instead, let's set aside the controversies and focus on the extraordinary possibilities that this technology offers us. After all, art has always been a field of experimentation and innovation, and MidJourney represents just the latest evolution of this fascinating journey.

The artistic use of artificial intelligence, the possibility of creating true works of art, captivates me. I am well aware of the ongoing debate between detractors who do not consider this tool a true generator of art and those who argue that this new technology offers an additional opportunity for artists. This passionate and intense debate reflects the complexity and depth of contemporary perceptions of art and creativity. However, I prefer not to dwell on these polemics.

Let's set aside the controversies and concentrate on the extraordinary possibilities that this technology offers. Art has always been a realm of experimentation and innovation, and MidJourney represents the latest evolution of this fascinating journey.

Imagine being able to combine different

artistic influences, mixing elements from various styles to create something truly unique and personal.

This is exactly what the "sref" function allows you to do. Through the use of specific codes, you can guide the Artificial Intelligence to produce images that precisely reflect the aesthetics you have in mind, without needing to write complex and detailed prompts.

Let's continue this exploration together, letting curiosity and creativity guide us. Midjourney has much to offer, and I am confident that, with the right understanding and application, you will find new ways to express your art and amaze the world with your creations.

How to Use a Midjourney sref Code?

To use a Midjourney "sref" code, simply include it in your prompt when generating an image. For example, you can type --sref 1996010 (where the number is hypothetical and can be replaced with any other value) to apply a specific effect. It is important that there is no space between -- and sref, and there is a space between sref and 1996010.

This process ensures that the resulting image adheres to the style defined by the sref code, making it easier to achieve consistent results. Below, you will find 132 suggestions that you can immediately apply to your creations.

Thus, the structure of a simple prompt becomes:

[Subject] --sref [Code] --ar [Proportions]:

Negli esempi allegati ho usato:

Female portrait, --sref 12345 --ar 2:3

Where the subject is a "female portrait" (I recommend always writing your request in English, as MJ, despite being able to understand over 100 languages, still needs to translate your prompt from the native language). The code after --sref can be any number you choose, and the value separated by the ":" after --ar indicates the width/height ratio.

Citations:

[1] https://sprinkleofai.com/how-to-use-the-new-midjourney-style-reference/
[2] https://docs.midjourney.com/docs/character-reference
[3] https://weirdwonderfulai.art/resources/a-guide-to-sref-style-reference-in-midjourney
[4] https://www.youtube.com/watch?v=K_rI5eh_WM0
[5] https://www.reddit.com/r/midjourney/comments/1bfh56i/is_sref_better_than_the_tuner_function/

prompt is a Latin term and means "request"

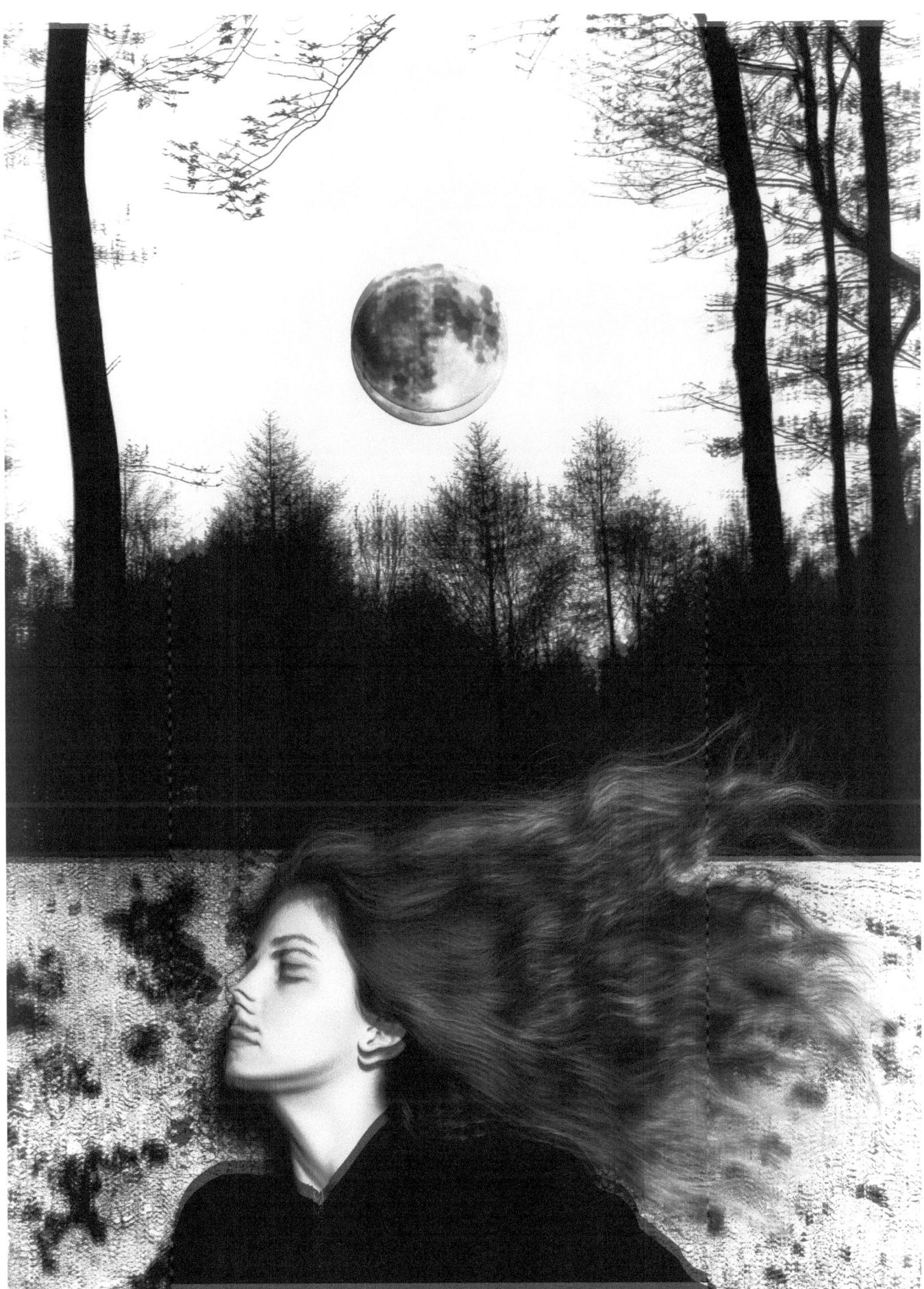

In this section you will find as many as 132 suggestions of "srf code " with the corresponding image generated by that value. You will only need to replicate it on MJ by changing the subject to get a similar graphical result.

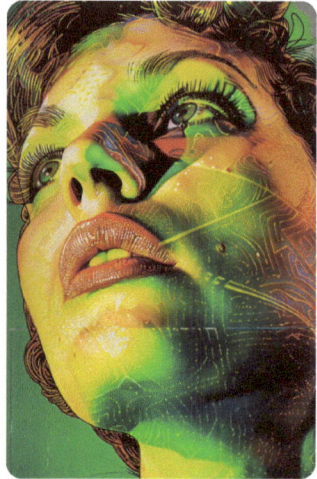

Female portrait --sref **619298202**

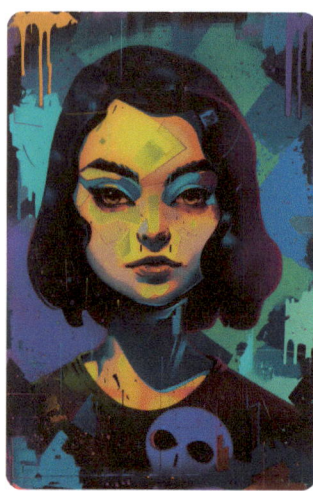

Female portrait --sref **8222885**

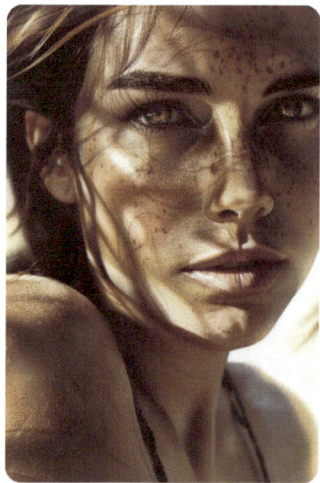

Female portrait --sref **2566504263**

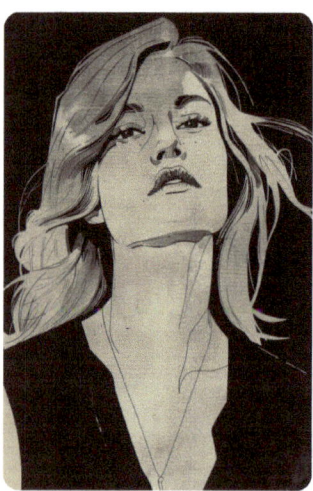

Female portrait --sref **625290222**

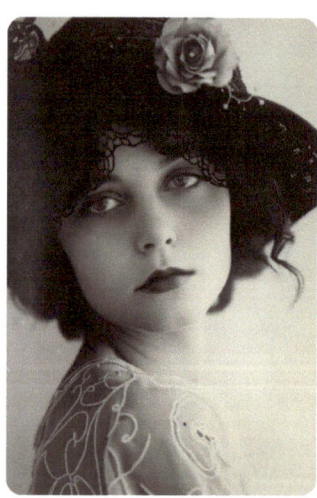

Female portrait --sref **1647818666**

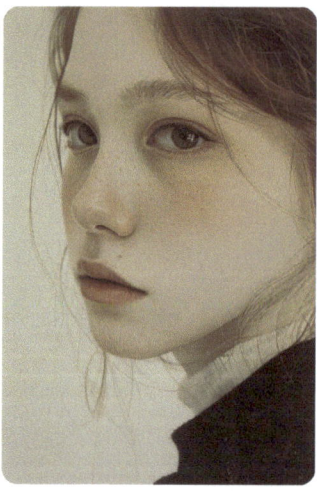

Female portrait --sref **3196338755**

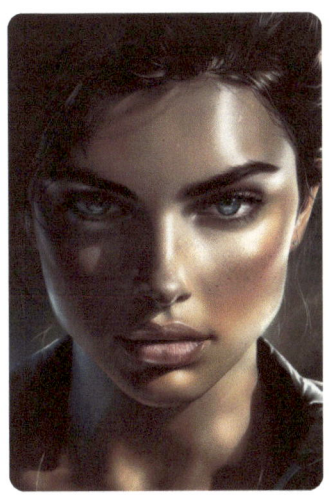

Female portrait --sref **522741134**

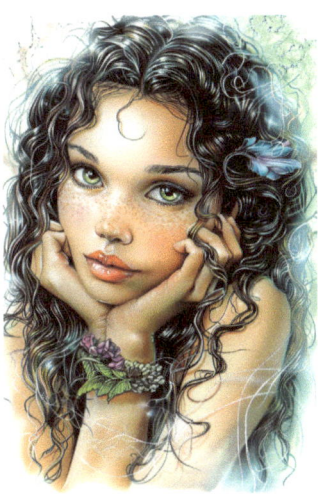

Female portrait --sref **2211420316**

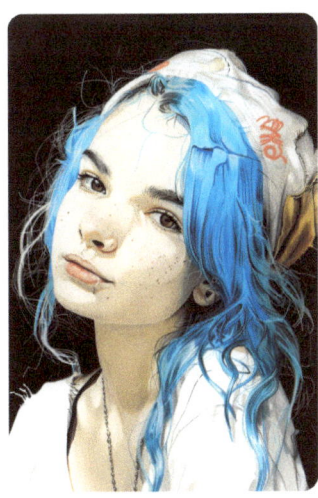

Female portrait --sref **4101609349**

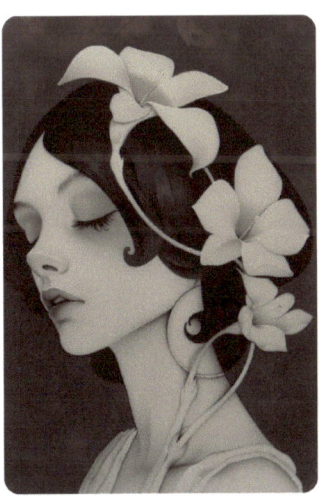

Female portrait --sref **738304901**

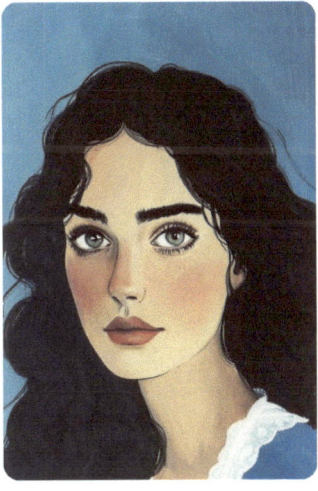

Female portrait --sref **1987682712**

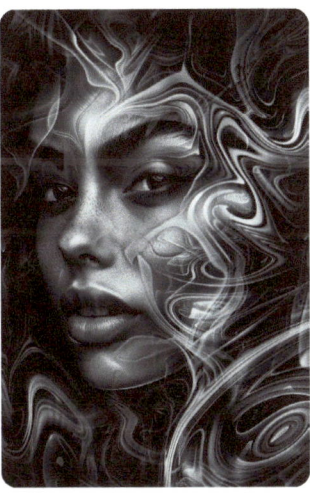

Female portrait --sref **4289481370**

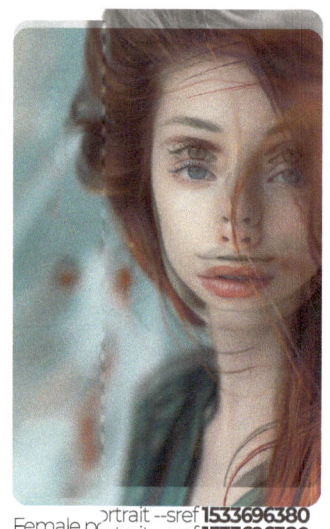

Female portrait --sref **1533696380**
Female portrait --sref **1533696380**

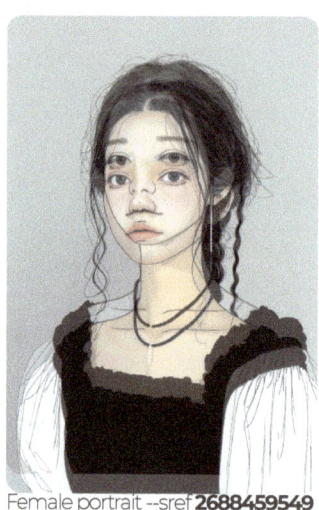

Female portrait --sref **2688459549**
Female portrait --sref **2688459549**

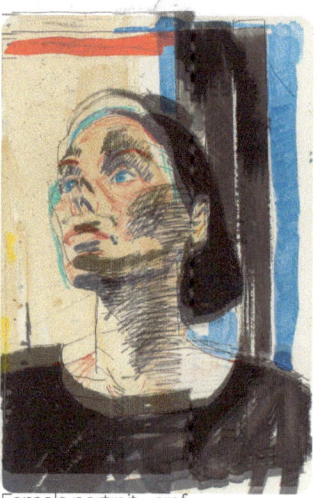

Female portrait --sref **3182922015**
Female portrait --sref **3182922015**

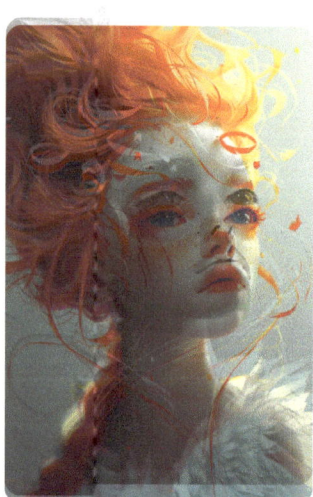

Female portrait --sref **3986566623**
Female portrait --sref **3986566623**

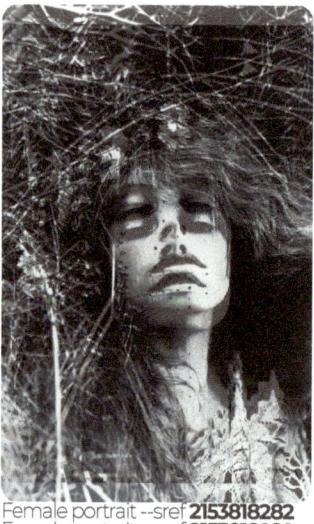

Female portrait --sref **2153818282**
Female portrait --sref **2153818282**

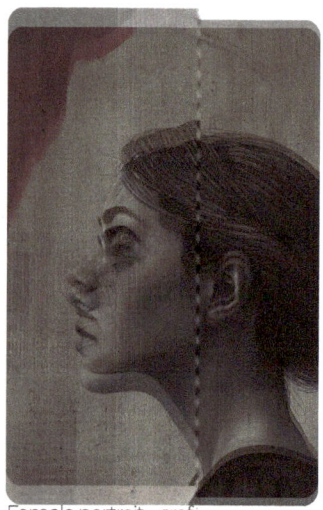

Female portrait --sref **3629271199**
Female portrait --sref **3629271199**

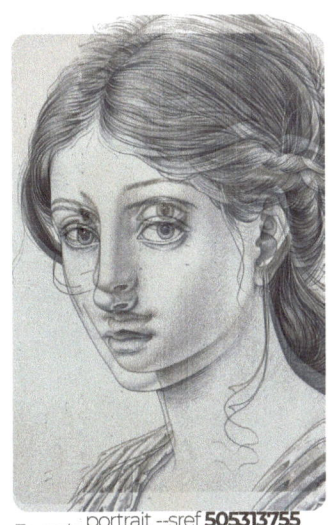

Female portrait --sref **505313755**
Female portrait --sref **505313755**

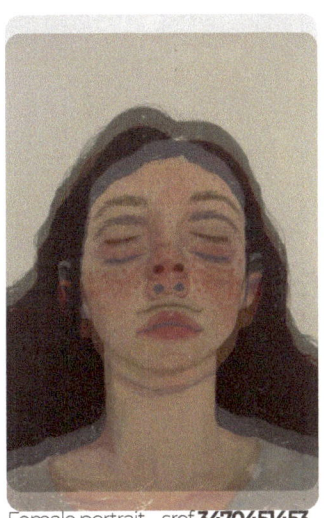

Female portrait --sref **3470451453**
Female portrait --sref **3470451453**

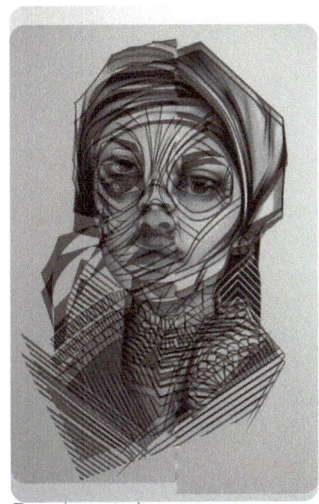

Female portrait --sr... **1764924675**
Female portrait --sref **1764924675**

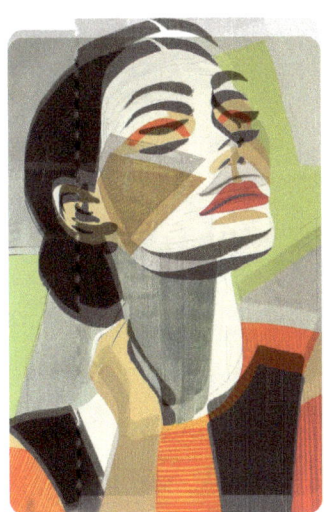

Female portrait --sref **415791975**
Female portrait --sref **415791975**

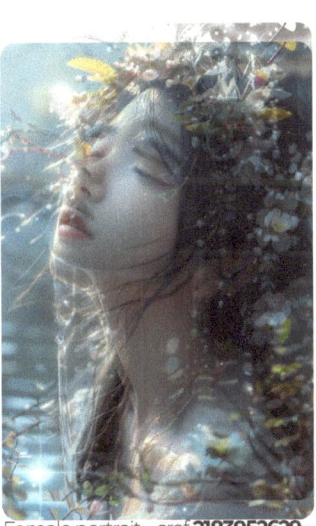

Female portrait --sref **2183952629**
Female portrait --sref **2183952629**

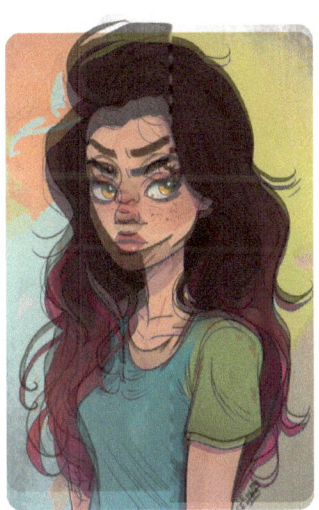

Female portrait --sr... **3255494320**
Female portrait --sref **3255494320**

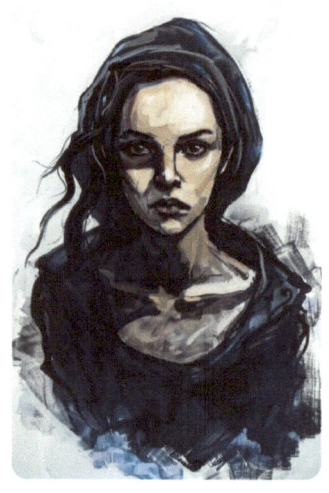
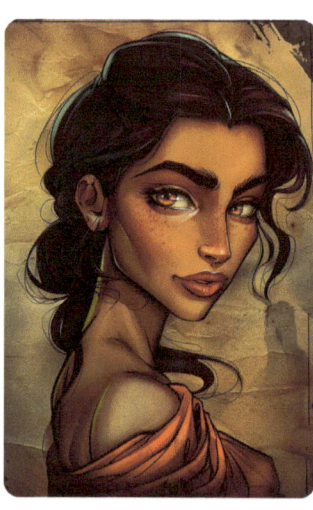
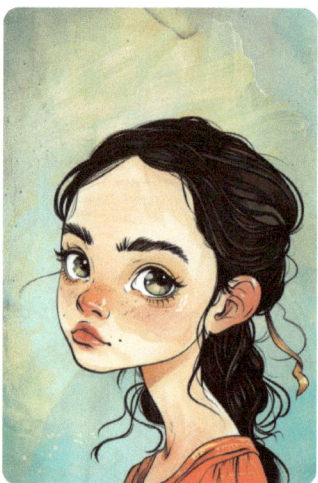

Female portrait --sref **813444700**   Female portrait --sref **1865885305**   Female portrait --sref **2177149847**

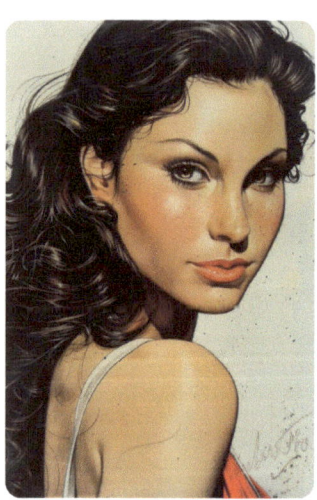
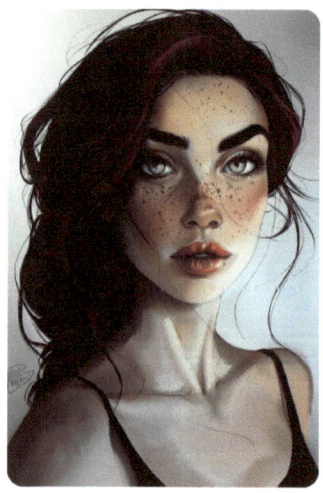
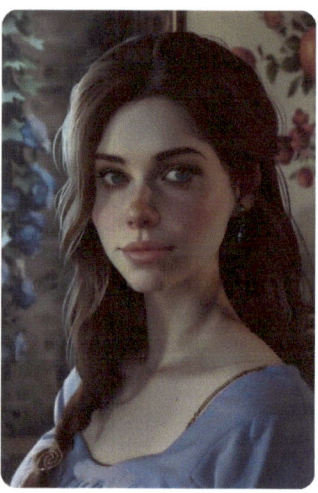

Female portrait --sref **4172073405**   Female portrait --sref **691842991**   Female portrait --sref **3493537063**

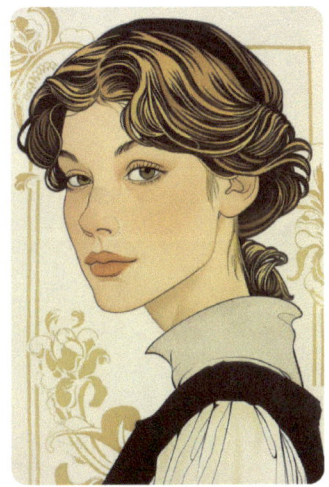

Female portrait --sref **2101577816**

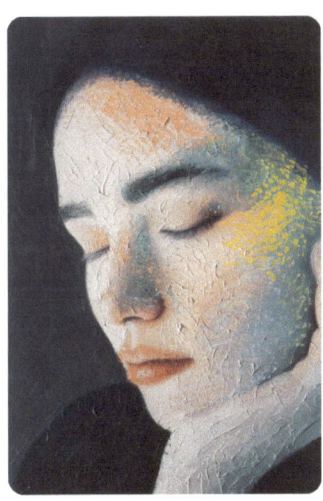

Female portrait --sref **3391195431**

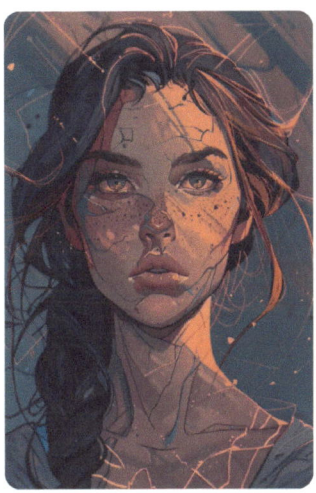

Female portrait --sref **3391195431**

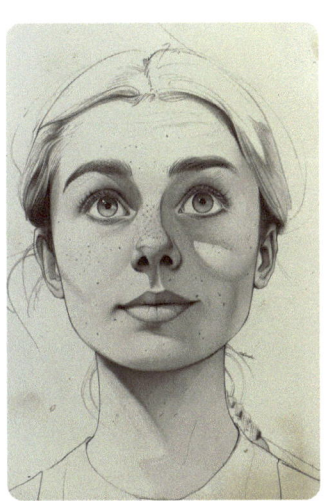

Female portrait --sref **2249018043**

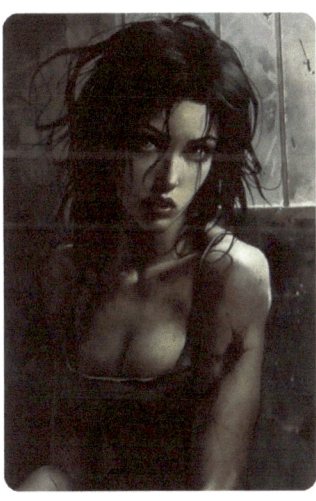

Female portrait --sref **319152602**

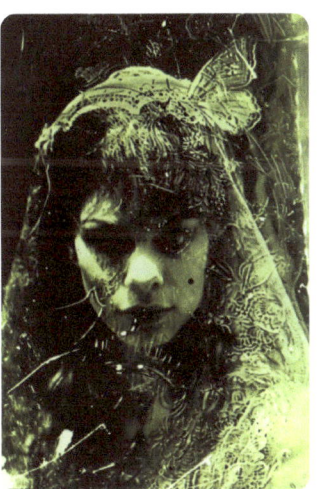

Female portrait --sref **2011452037**

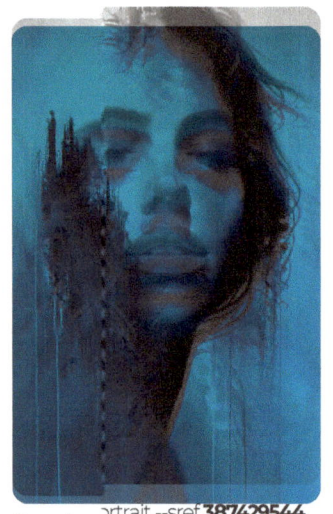

Female portrait --sref **387429544**
Female portrait --sref **387429544**

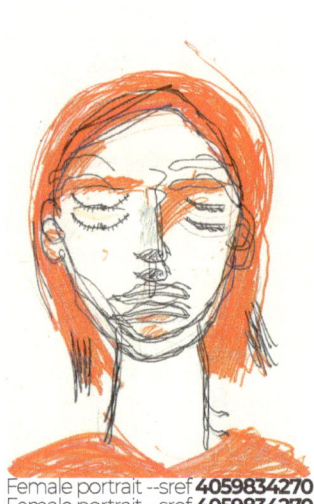

Female portrait --sref **4059834270**
Female portrait --sref **4059834270**

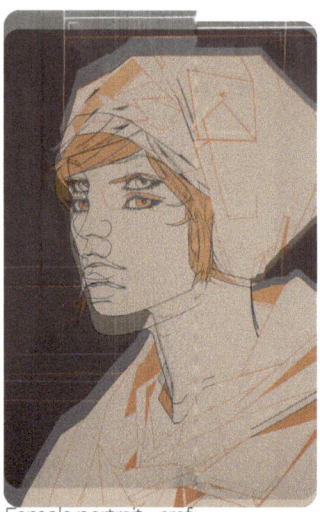

Female portrait --sref **1635781360**
Female portrait --sref **1635781360**

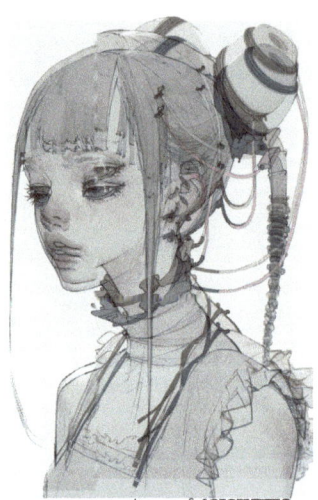

Female portrait --sref **4212115738**
Female portrait --sref **4212115738**

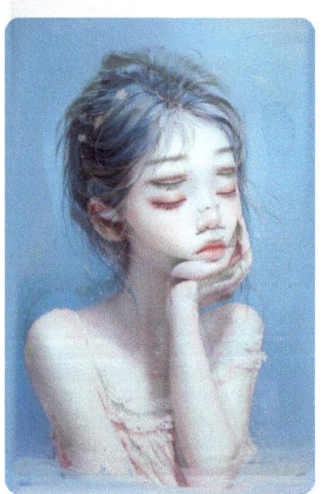

Female portrait --sref **1839784916**
Female portrait --sref **1839784916**

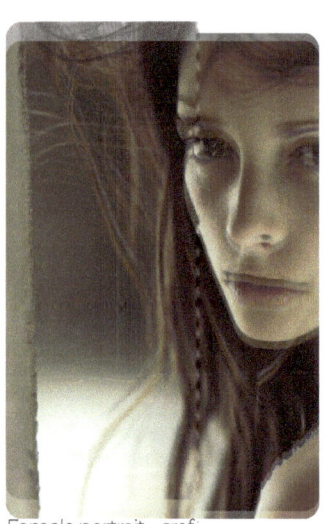

Female portrait --sref **3200**
Female portrait --sref **3200**

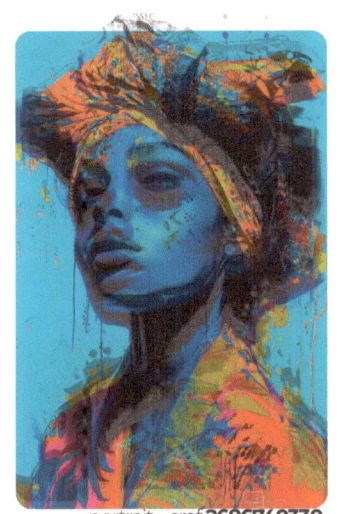

Female portrait --sref **2686740330**
Female portrait --sref **2686740330**

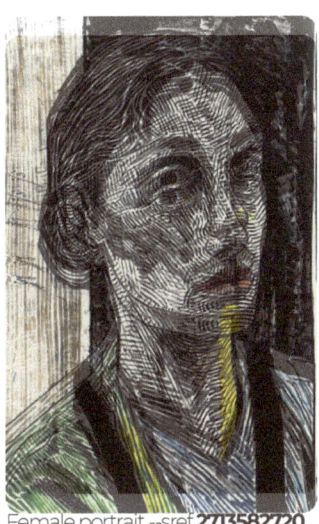

Female portrait --sref **2713582720**
Female portrait --sref **2713582720**

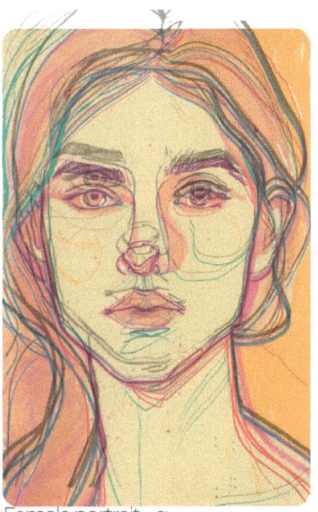

Female portrait --sr... ...ef **3035259247**
Female portrait --sref **3035259247**

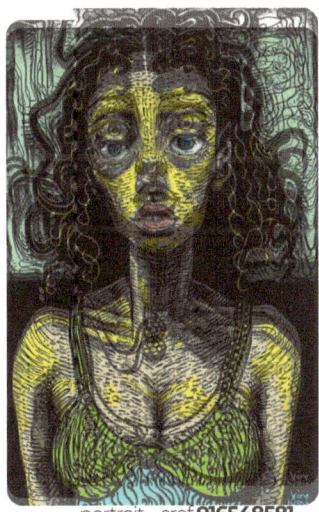

Female portrait --sref **916548581**
Female portrait --sref **916548581**

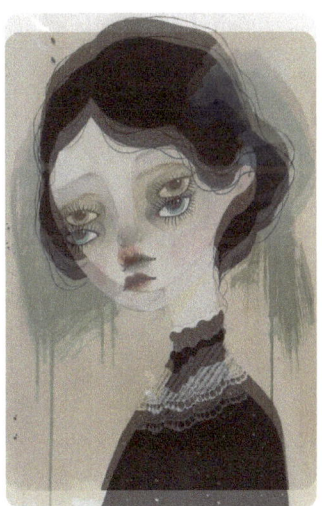

Female portrait --sref **3761239642**
Female portrait --sref **3761239642**

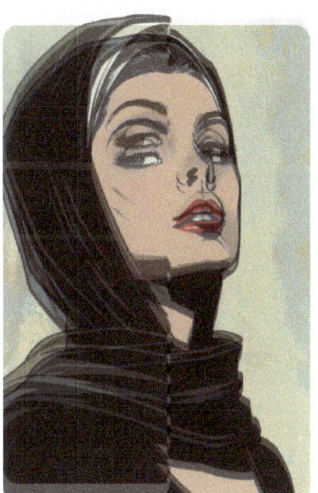

Female portrait --sr... ...ef **4294967295**
Female portrait --sref **4294967295**

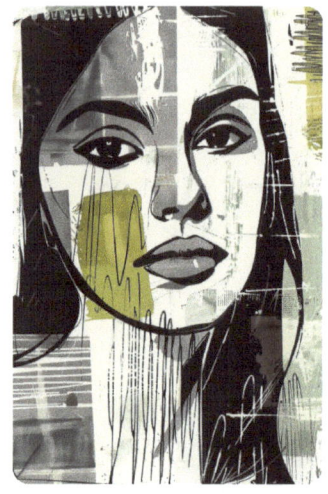

Female portrait --sref **2472621543**

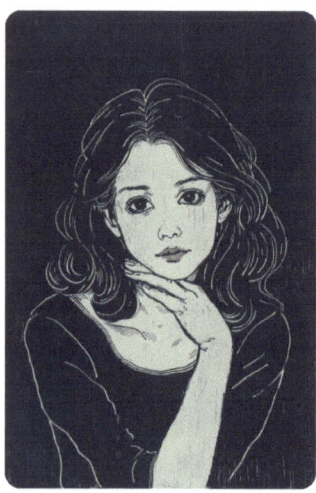

Female portrait --sref **3419166119**

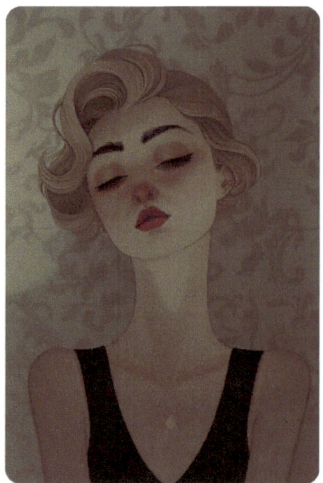

Female portrait --sref **5302024**

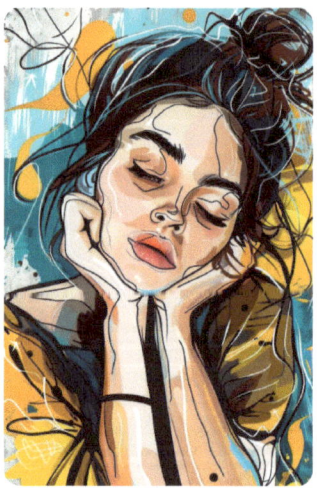

Female portrait --sref **20240627**

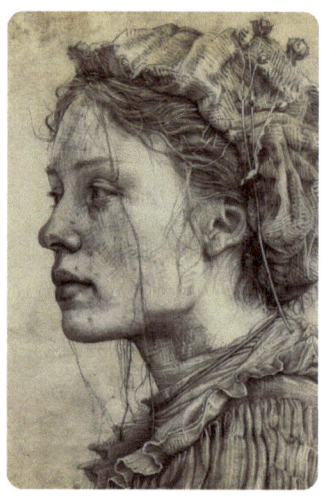

Female portrait --sref **776144174**

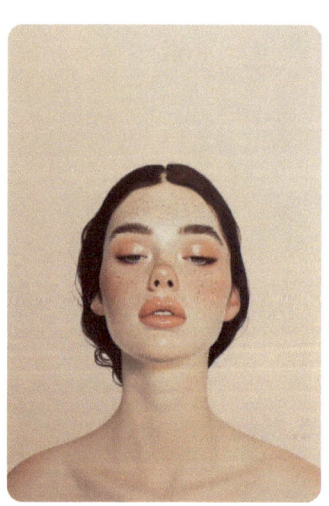

Female portrait --sref **577817196**

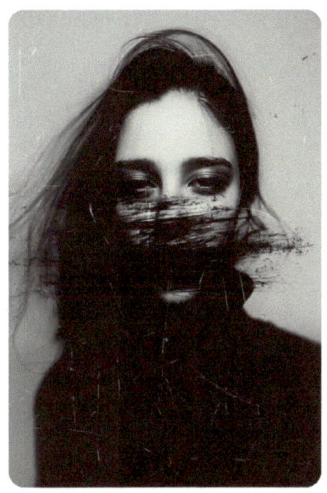

Female portrait --sref **373**

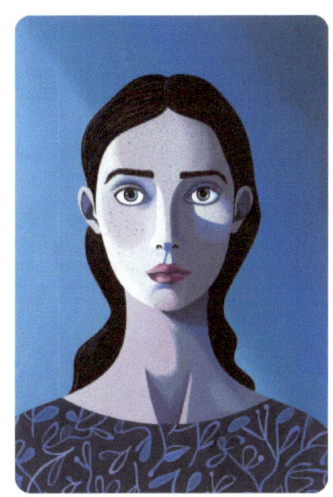

Female portrait --sref **783**

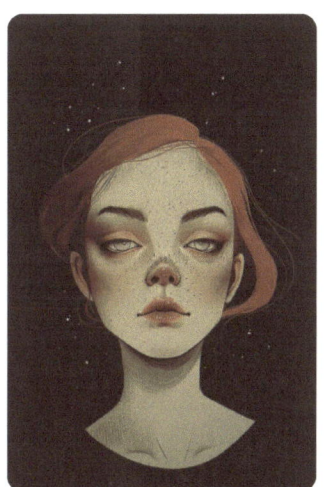

Female portrait --sref **24000022**

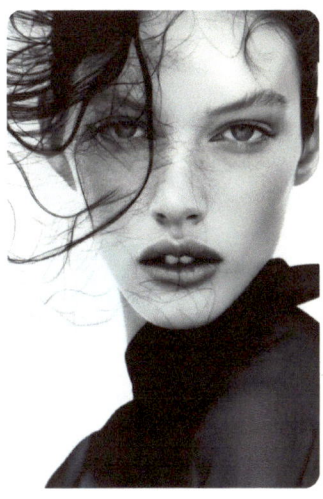

Female portrait --sref **557**

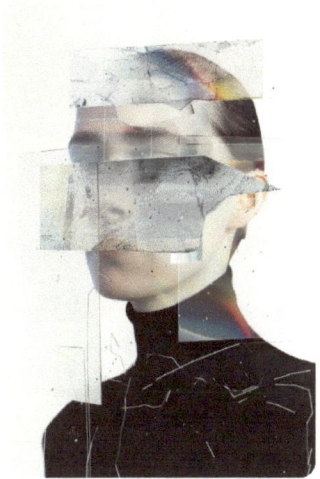

Female portrait --sref **3844938906**

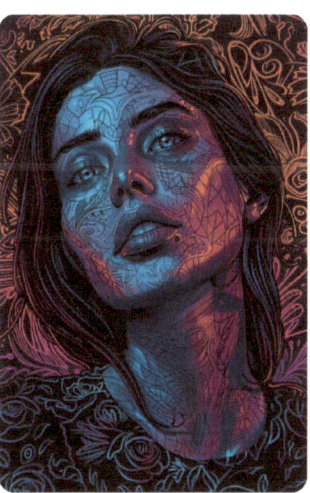

Female portrait --sref **1031796828**

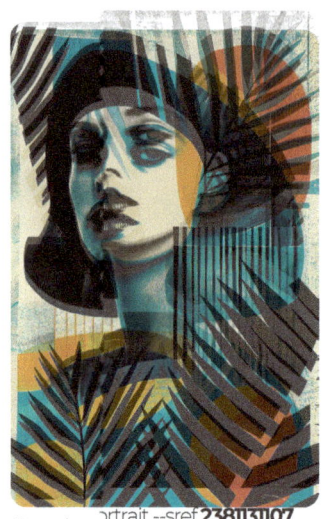

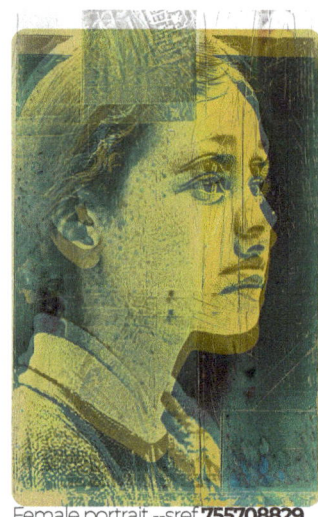

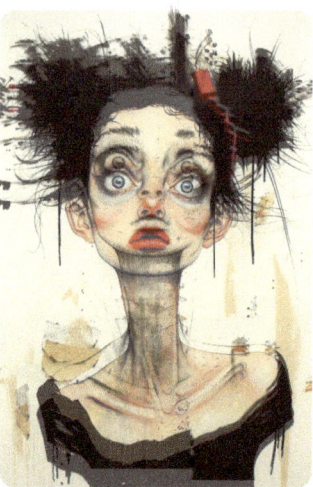

Female portrait --sref **2381131107**
Female portrait --sref **2381131107**

Female portrait --sref **755708829**
Female portrait --sref **755708829**

Female portrait --sref **4052966870**
Female portrait --sref **4052966870**

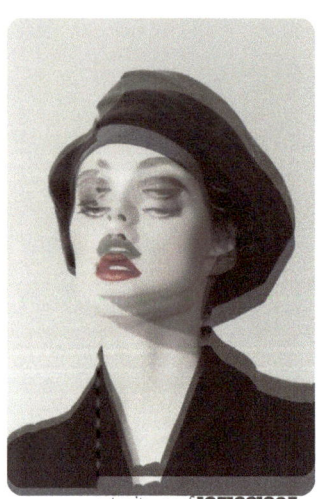

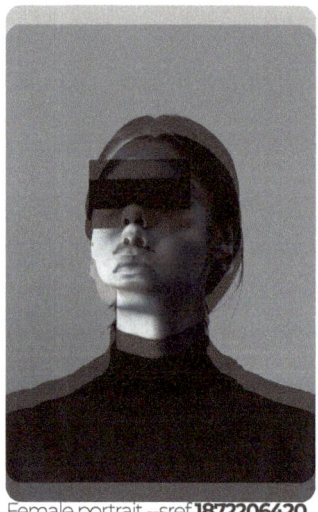

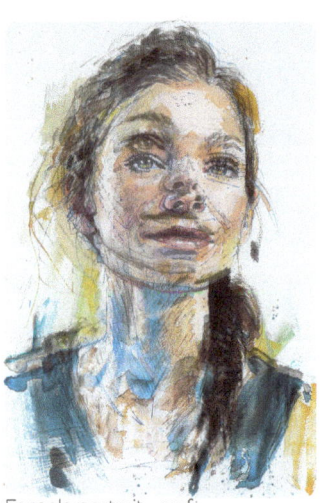

Female portrait --sref **1851881805**
Female portrait --sref **1851881805**

Female portrait --sref **1872206420**
Female portrait --sref **1872206420**

Female portrait --sref **1975653052**
Female portrait --sref **1975653052**

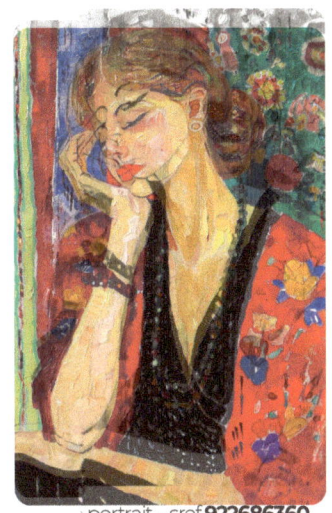

Female portrait --sref **922686360**
Female portrait --sref **922686360**

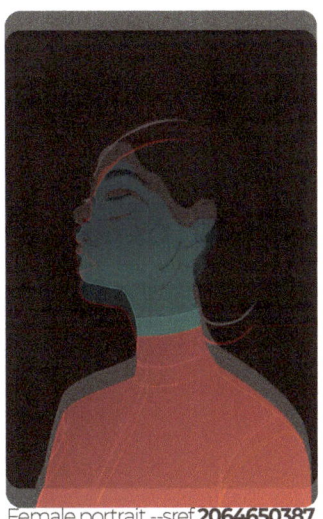

Female portrait --sref **2064650387**
Female portrait --sref **2064650387**

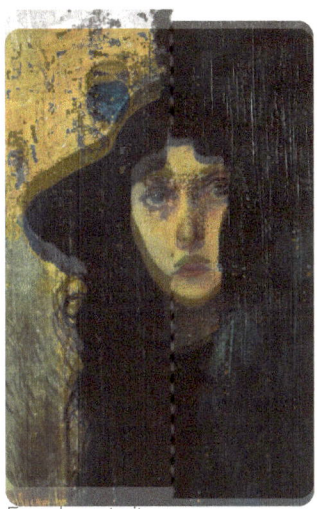

Female portrait --sref **3701757032**
Female portrait --sref **3701757032**

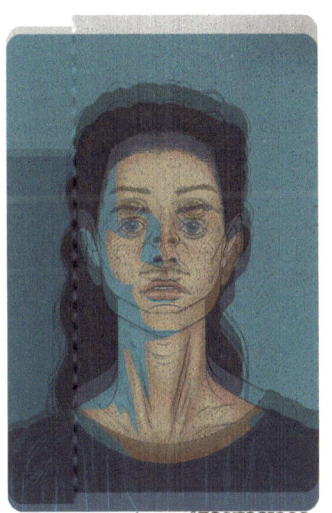

Female portrait --sref **3897881209**
Female portrait --sref **3897881209**

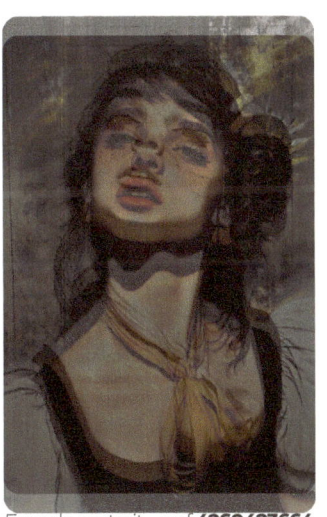

Female portrait --sref **4260423664**
Female portrait --sref **4260423664**

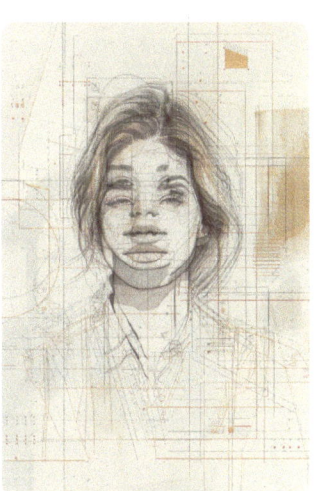

Female portrait --sref **1687696634**
Female portrait --sref **1687696634**

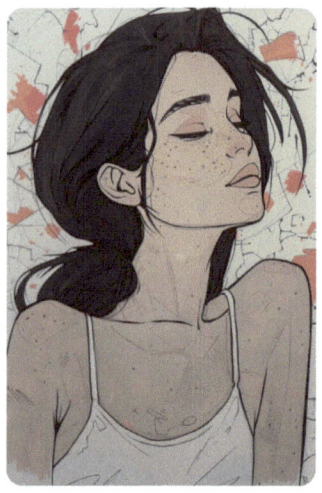

Female portrait --sref **1459128765**

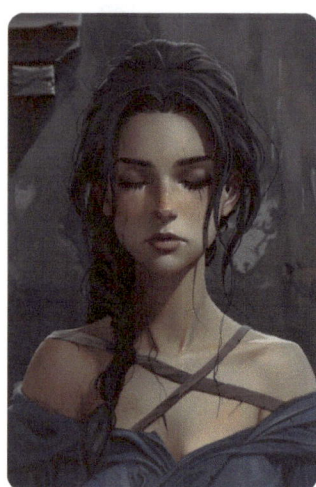

Female portrait --sref **1689584363**

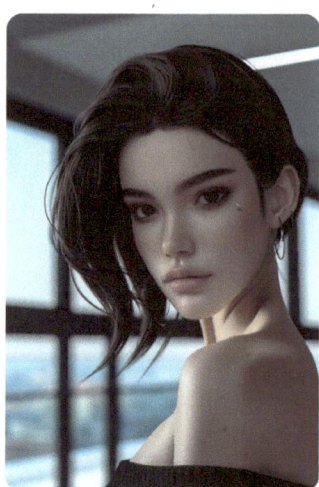

Female portrait --sref **1249996062**

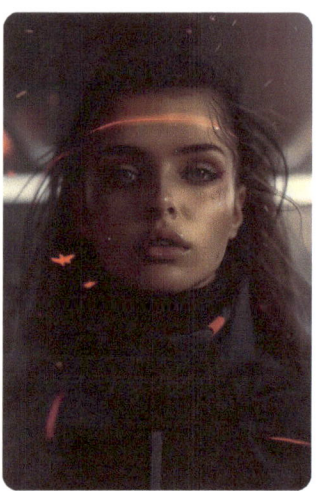

Female portrait --sref **642458668**

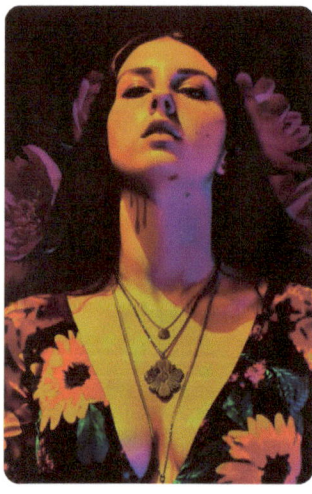

Female portrait --sref **4055354536**

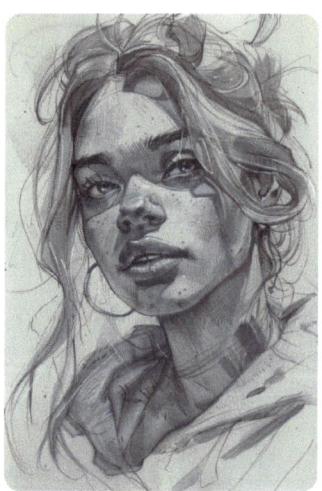

Female portrait --sref **20240616**

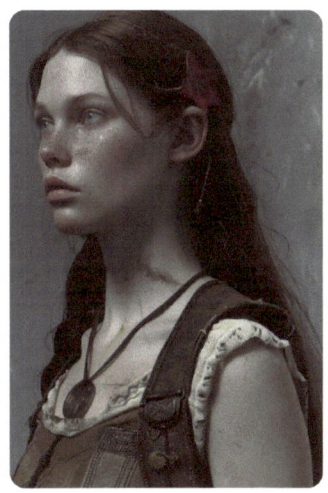

Female portrait --sref **647773822**

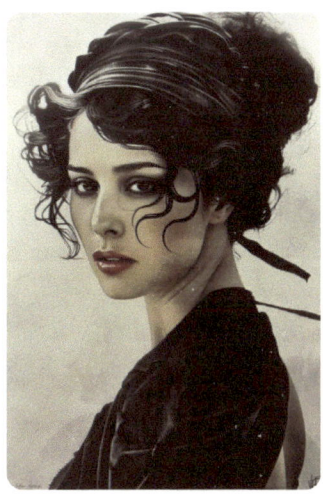

Female portrait --sref **2472004205**

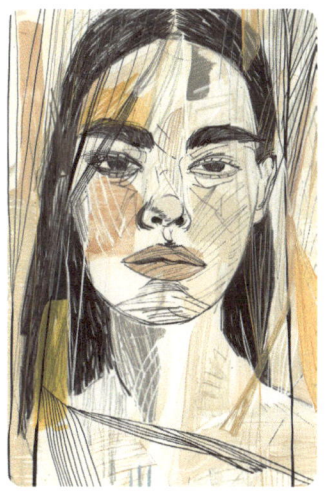

Female portrait --sref **1961992465**

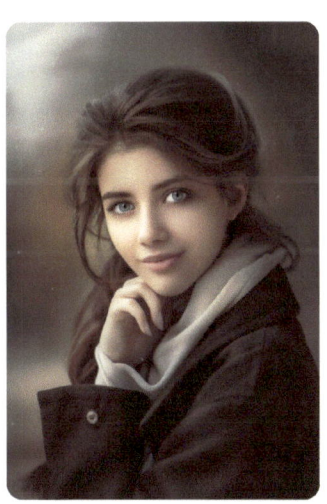

Female portrait --sref **3693830251**

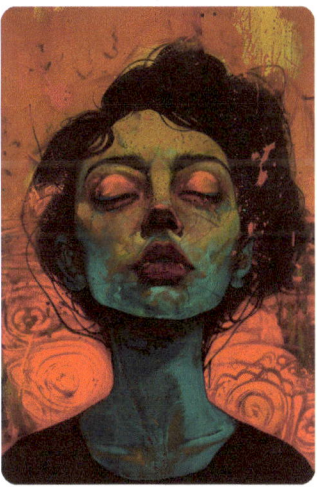

Female portrait --sref **3240549077**

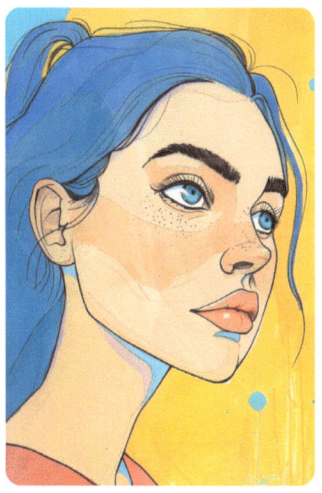

Female portrait --sref **2148072434**

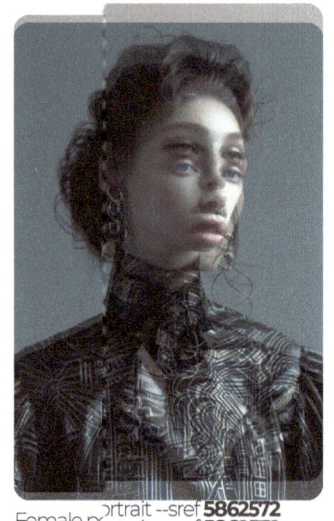

Female portrait --sref **5862572**

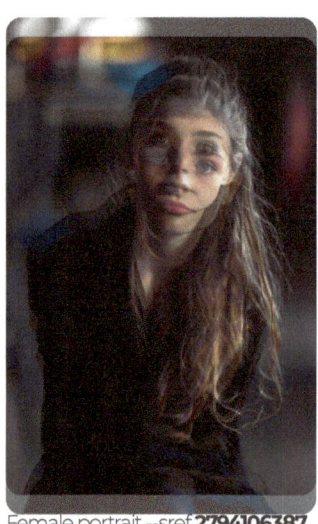

Female portrait --sref **2794106387**

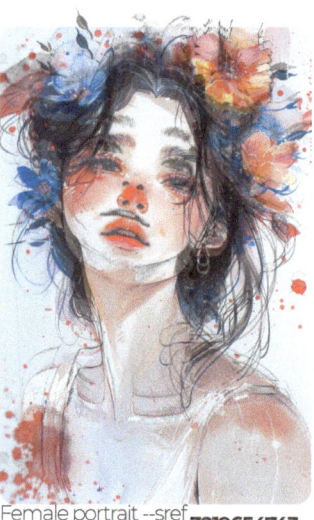

Female portrait --sref **3219654743**

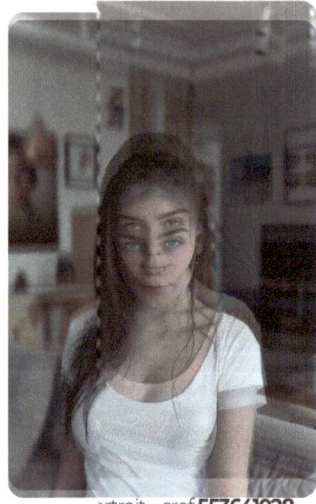

Female portrait --sref **553641028**

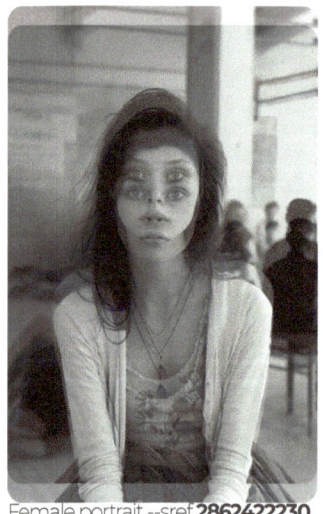

Female portrait --sref **2862422230**

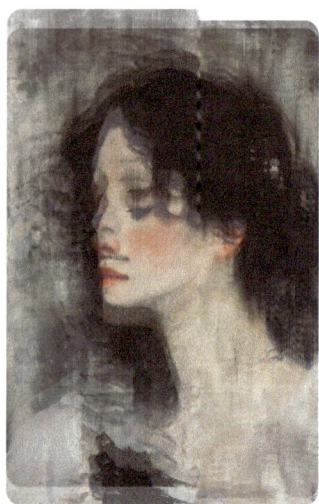

Female portrait --sref **2069007749**

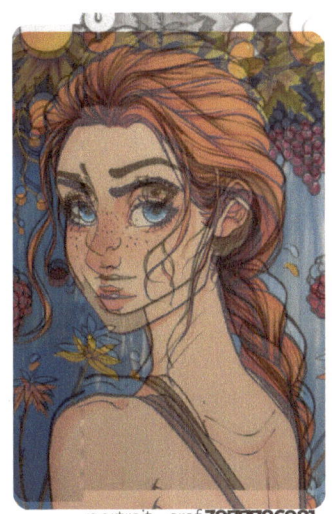

Female portrait --sref **3977786981**
Female portrait --sref **3977786981**

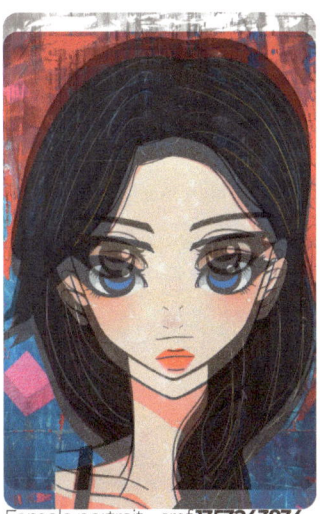

Female portrait --sref **1353243834**
Female portrait --sref **1353243834**

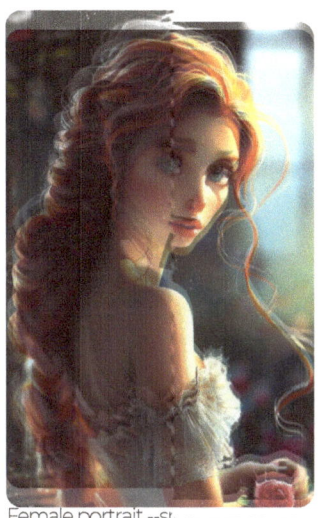

Female portrait --sr... **1233366278**
Female portrait --sref **1233366278**

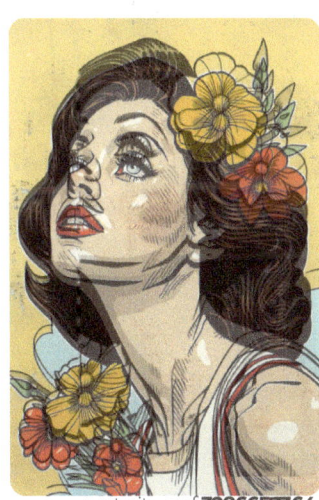

Female portrait --sref **3286657364**
Female portrait --sref **3286657364**

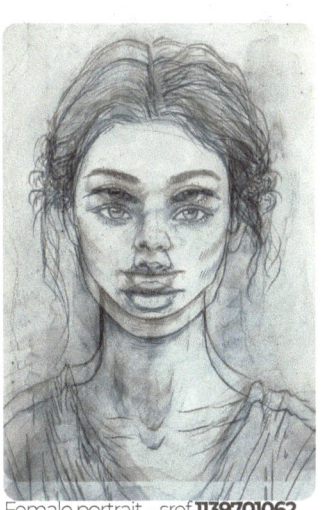

Female portrait --sref **1139701062**
Female portrait --sref **1139701062**

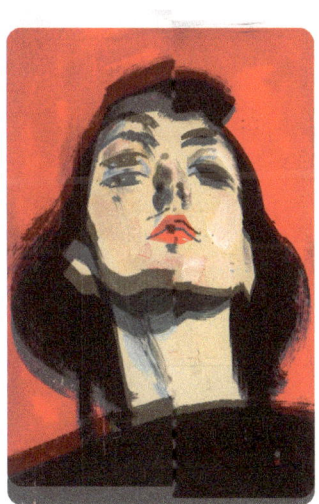

Female portrait --sr... **3359081976**
Female portrait --sref **3359081976**

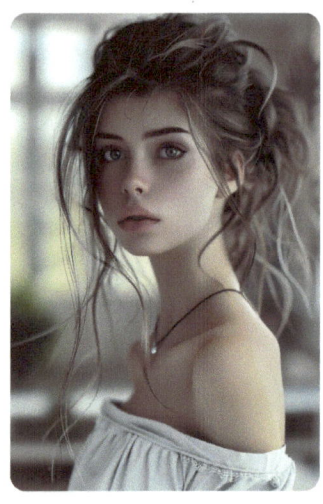

Female portrait --sref **335902878**

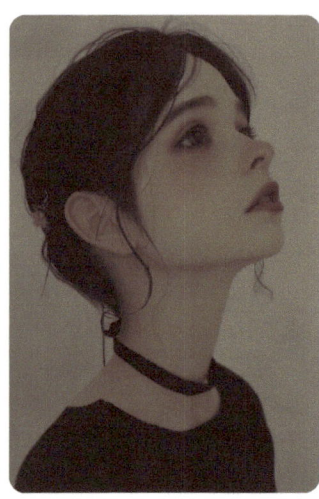

Female portrait --sref **3008609073**

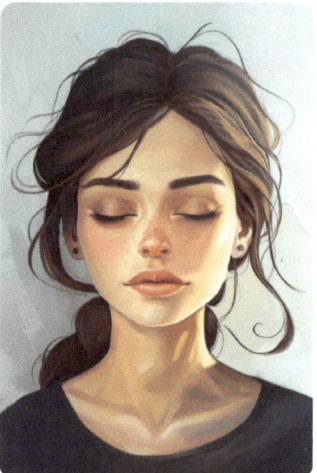

Female portrait --sref **1046774168**

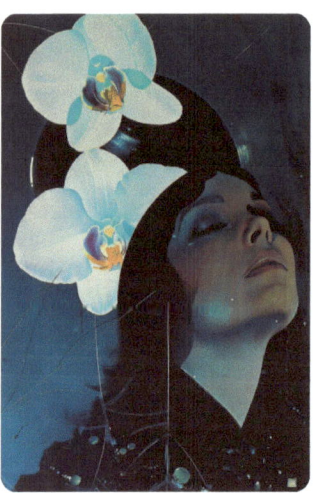

Female portrait --sref **1856301189**

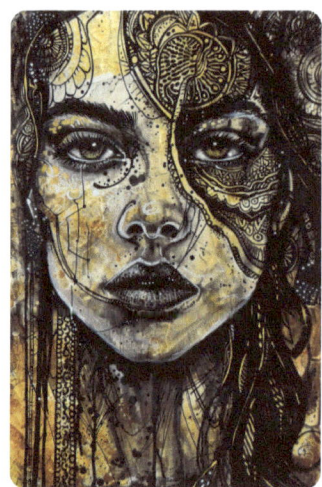

Female portrait --sref **1140670621**

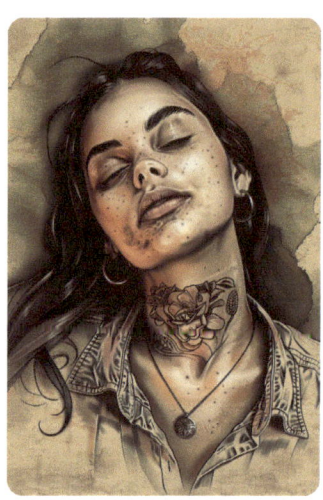

Female portrait --sref **447239176**

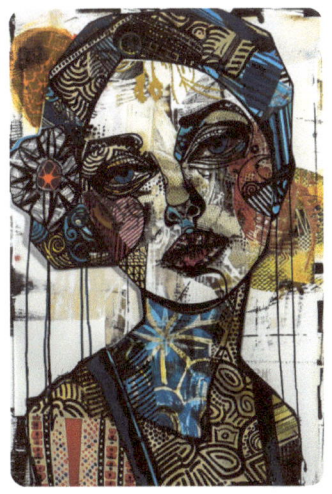

Female portrait --sref **970869276**

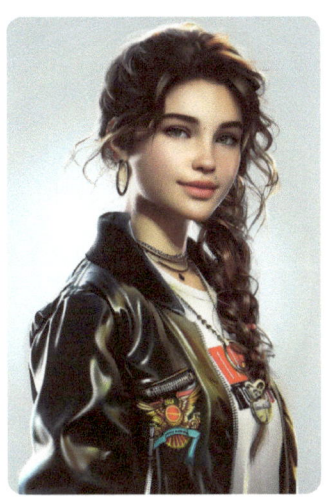

Female portrait --sref **970869276**

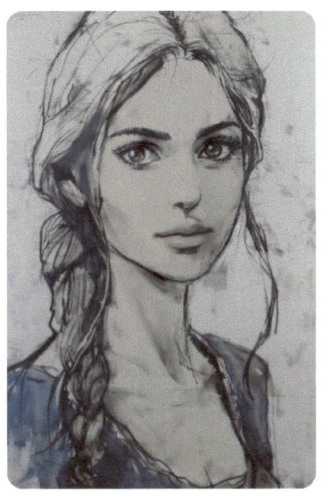

Female portrait --sref **1731589174**

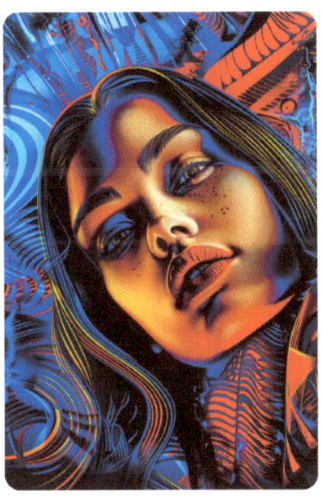

Female portrait --sref **881815916**

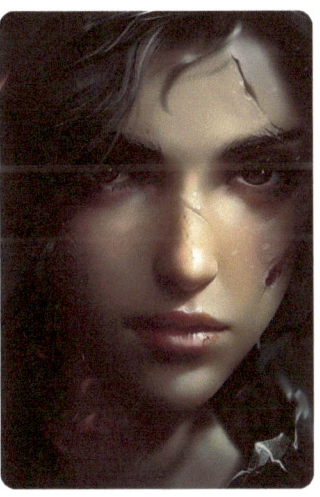

Female portrait --sref **1946802936**

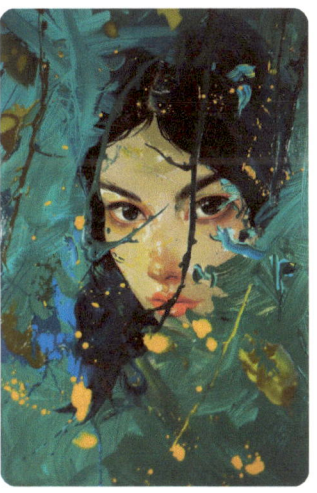

Female portrait --sref **2373237091**

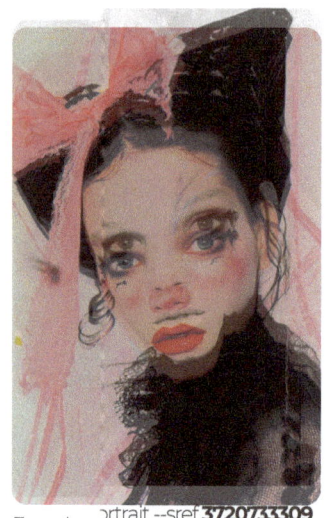

Female portrait --sref **3720733309**

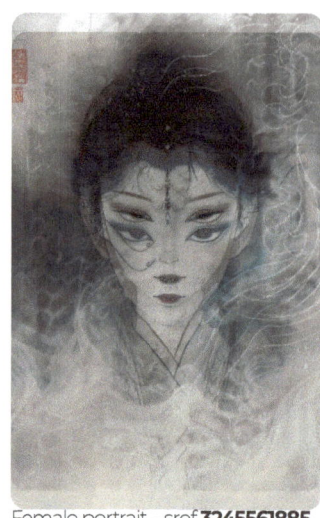

Female portrait --sref **3245561885**

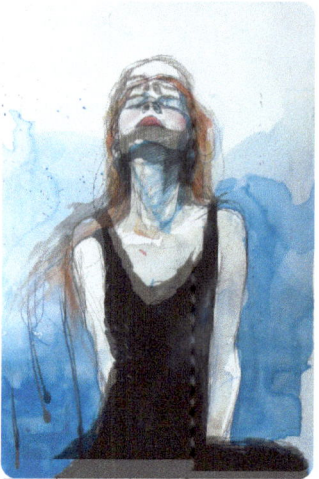

Female portrait --sref **4077003879**

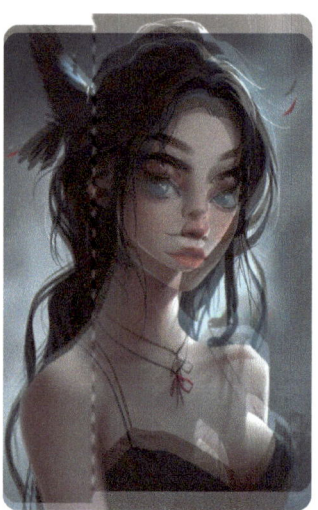

Female portrait --sref **2080917109**

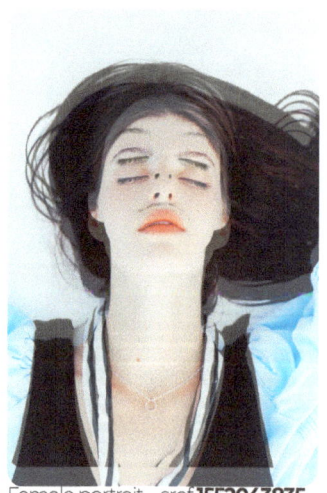

Female portrait --sref **1552043835**

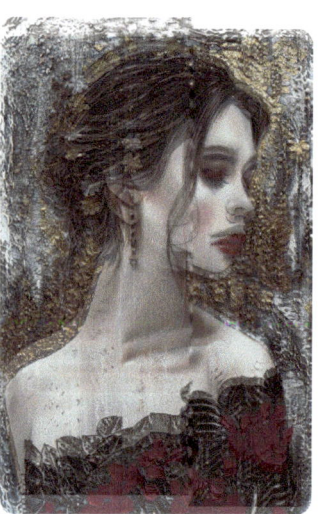

Female portrait --sref **3490687635**

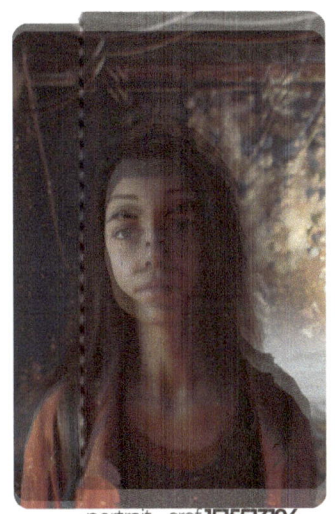

Female portrait --sref **1515513194**
Female portrait --sref **1515513194**

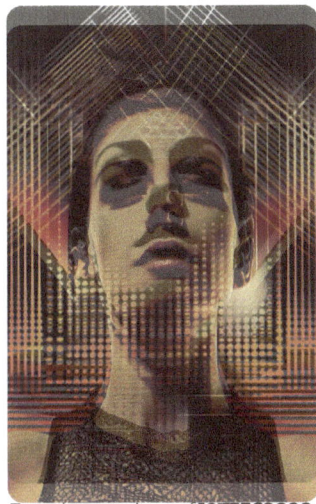

Female portrait --sref **1075569000**
Female portrait --sref **1075569000**

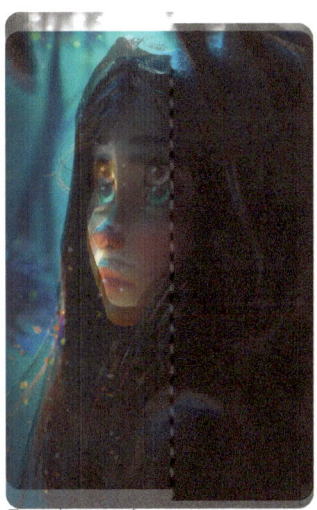

Female portrait --sr_f **1018345985**
Female portrait --sref **1018345985**

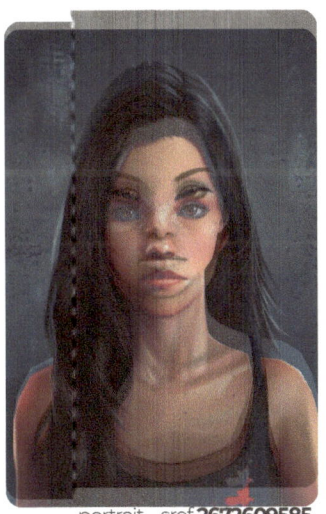

Female portrait --sref **2672609585**
Female portrait --sref **2672609585**

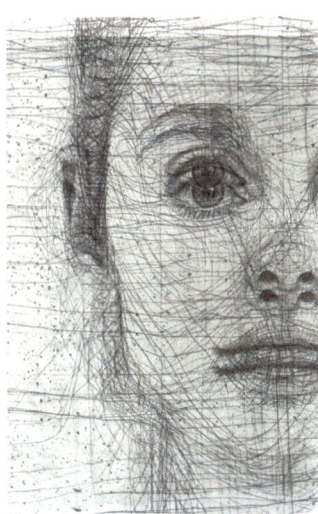

Female portrait --sref **527658160**
Female portrait --sref **527658160**

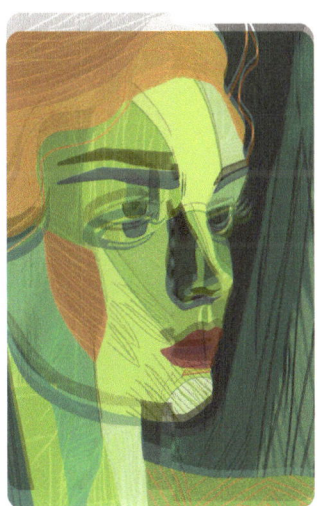

Female portrait --sr_f **1896223148**
Female portrait --sref **1896223148**

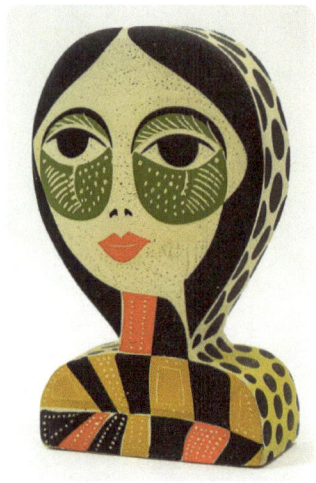

Female portrait --sref **3260027413**

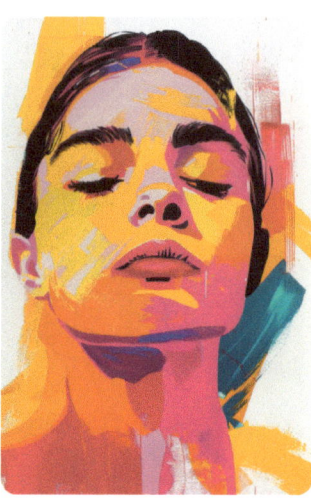

Female portrait --sref **4140967924**

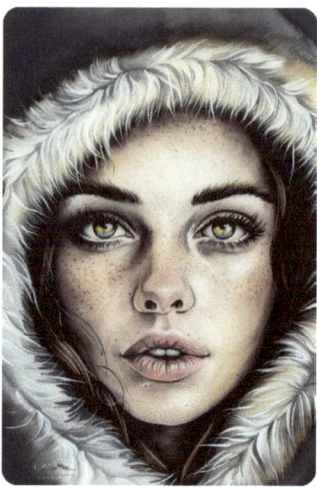

Female portrait --sref **2255789302**

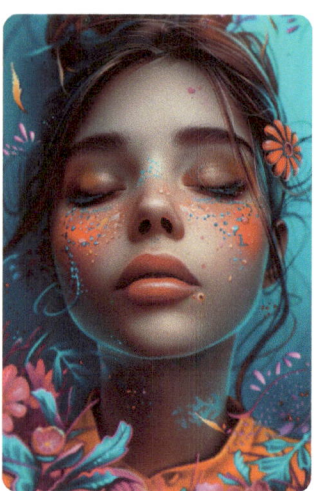

Female portrait --sref **769358618**

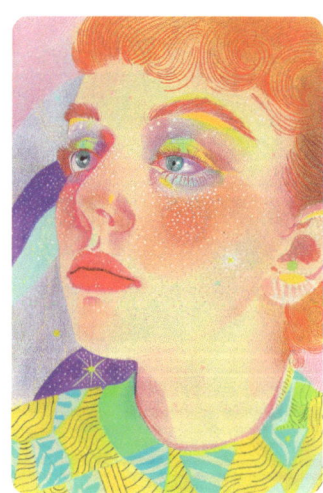

Female portrait --sref **263540803**

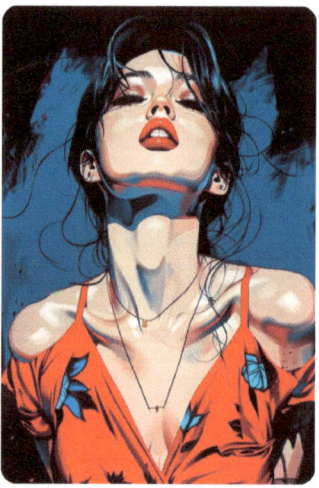

Female portrait --sref **2376784914**

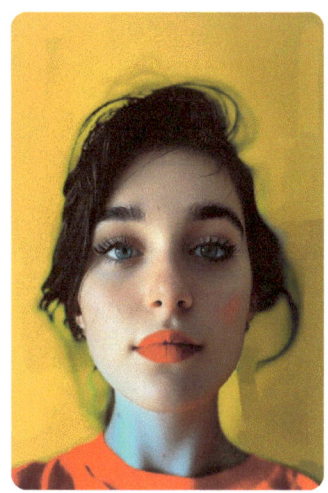

Female portrait --sref **3927322257**

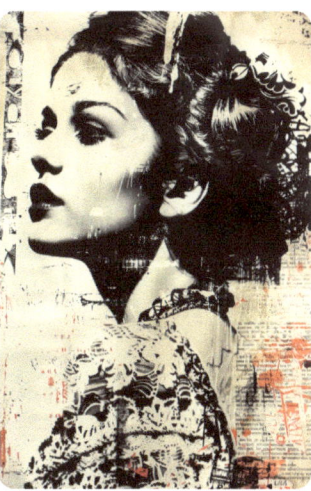

Female portrait --sref **2438426728**

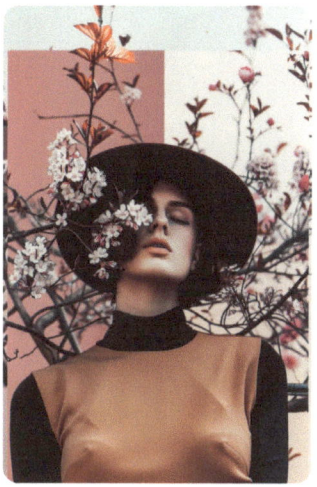

Female portrait --sref **952191169**

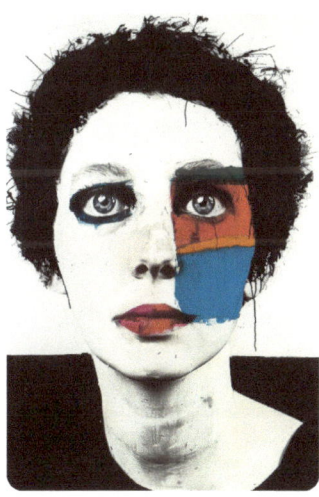

Female portrait --sref **1310231151**

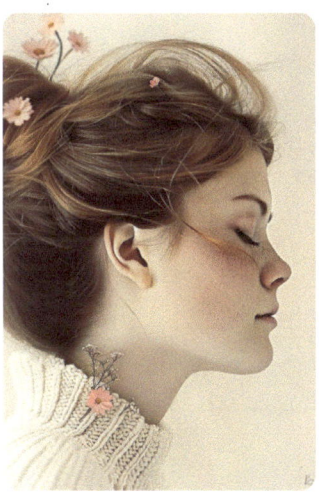

Female portrait --sref **1232155288**

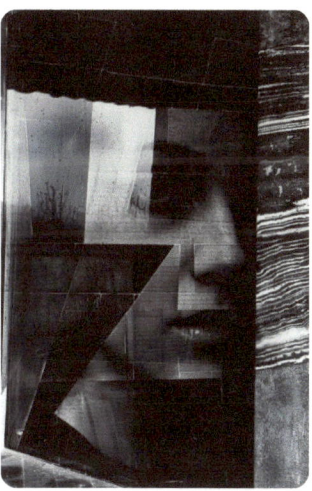

Female portrait --sref **1451687722**

Now I'll let you in on a secret that will allow you to further customize your search: try typing "--sref random" without entering the code. This way you will ask MJ to try one for you. "Random" will be transformed into a random numeric value.

Alternatively, try using particular numbers, your date of birth, the time, the year, your phone number, and whatever other cues come from your mathematical imagination. In the examples below I have simply used progressive numbering from 1 to 12.

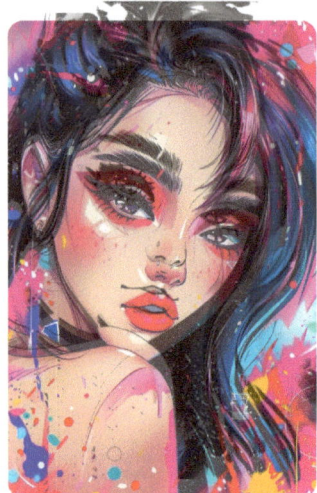

Female portrait --sref **1**

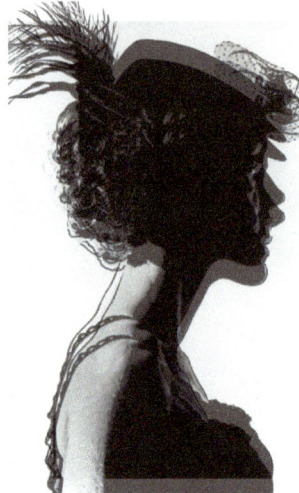

Female portrait --sref **2**

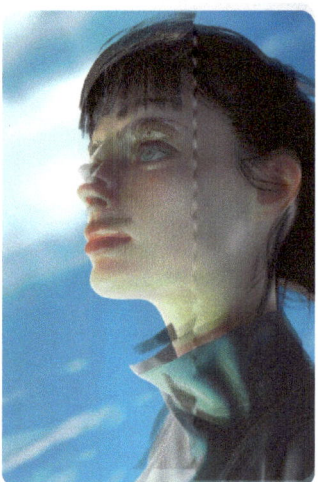

Female portrait --sref **3**

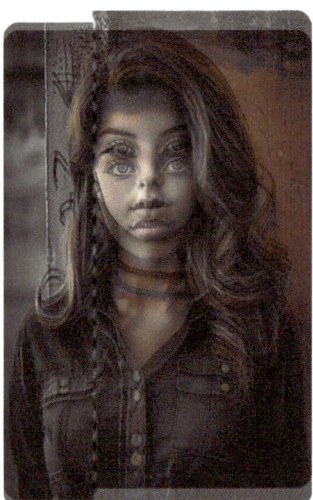

Female portrait --sref **4**

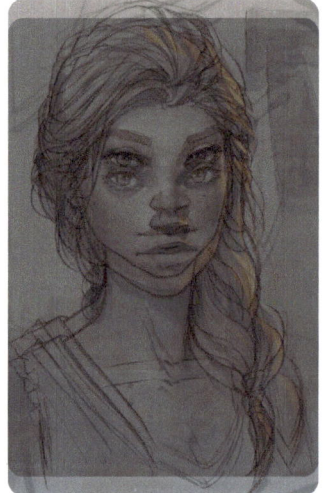

Female portrait --sref **5**

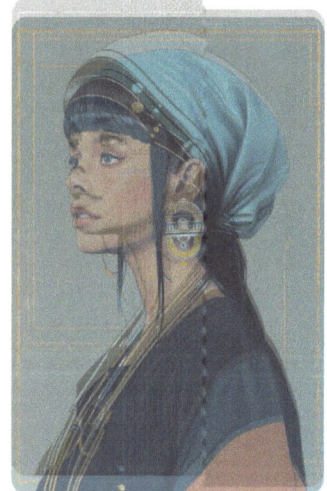

Female portrait --sref **6**

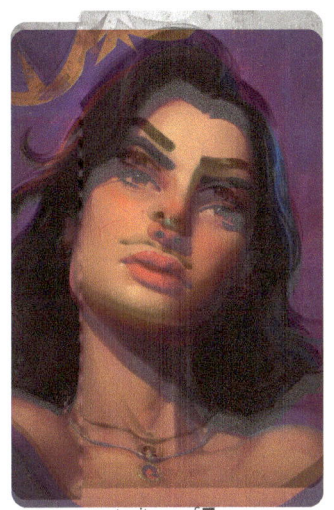

Female portrait --sref **7**
Female portrait --sref **7**

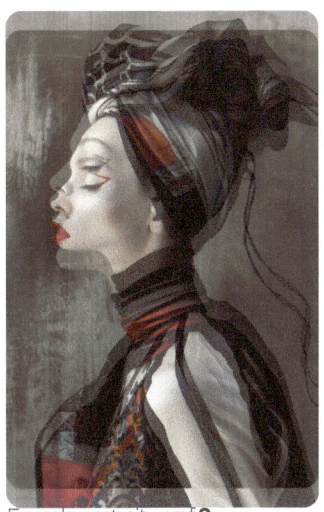

Female portrait --sref **8**
Female portrait --sref **8**

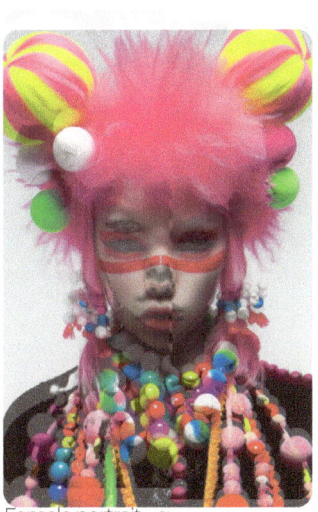

Female portrait --sr...
Female portrait --sref **9**

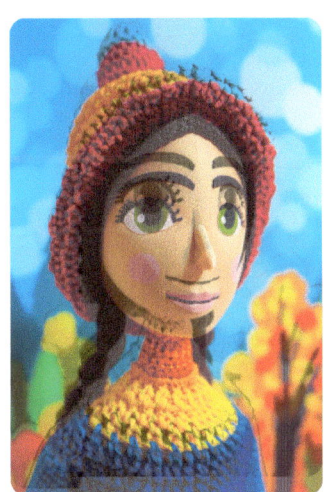

Female portrait --sref **10**
Female portrait --sref **10**

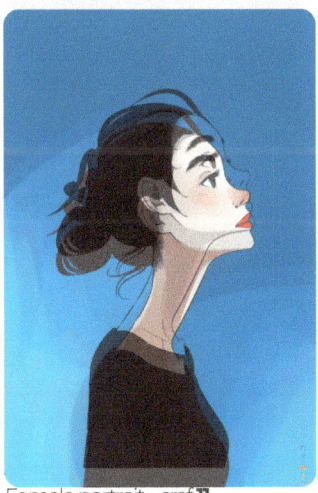

Female portrait --sref **11**
Female portrait --sref **11**

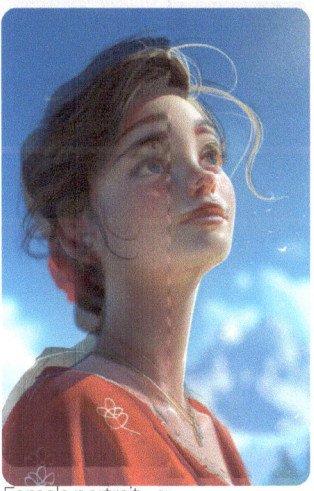

Female portrait --sr...
Female portrait --sref **12**

By getting to this point you will have understood the potential of using code (I ask that, if you do not get the desired result on the first try, you try several times). Now try simply changing the subject of the prompt to customize your request.

Codice scelto: **1896223148**

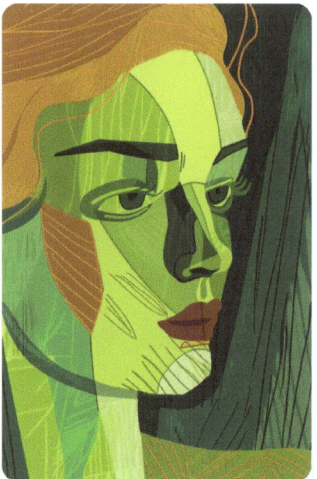

Female portrait --sref **1896223148**

Soggetto: **Dream**

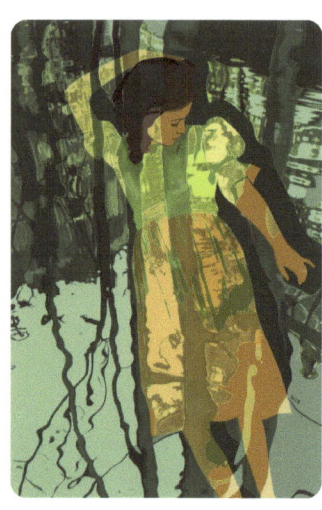

Dream --sref **1896223148**

Soggetto: **Landscape**

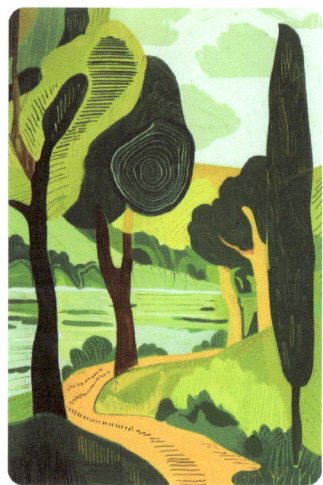

Landscape --sref **1896223148**

Soggetto: **City**

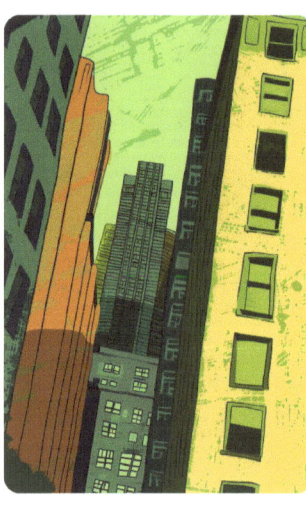

City --sref **769358618**

Soggetto: **Fish**

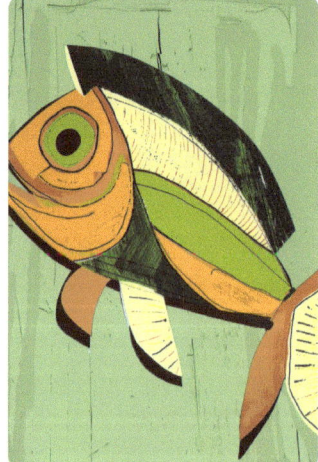

Fish --sref **263540803**

Soggetto: **Boy**

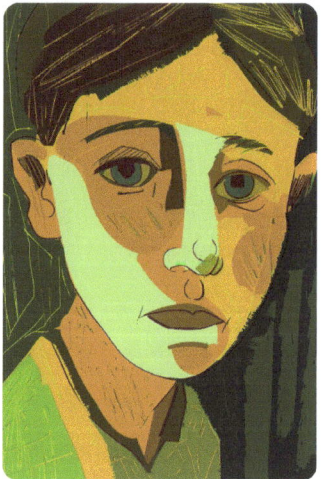

Boy --sref **2376784914**

So now you can, after choosing the code you like, get images that are consistent with each other, so you can illustrate a children's book, create a graphic novel, or create works to sell or hang in your home.

In the examples on this page, I have also added the parameter "**in the style of**" followed by the name of a famous artist to further enhance your request and generate a unique image.

Codice scelto: **1896223148**

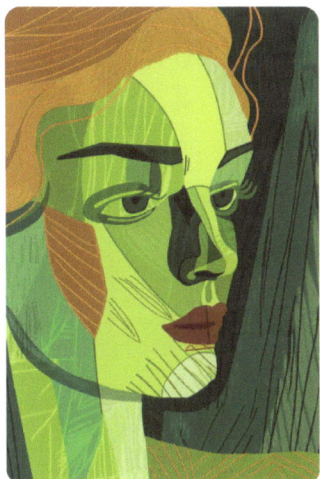

Female portrait --sref **1896223148**

Nello stile di: **Picasso**

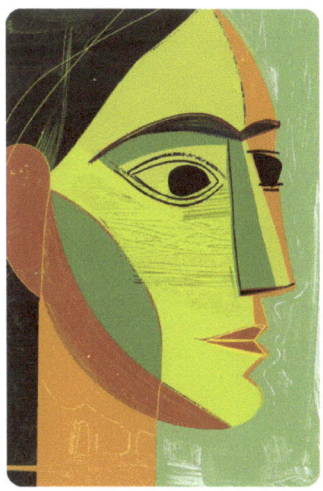

Female portrait, in the style of **Picasso** --sref 1896223148

Nello stile di: **Basquiat**

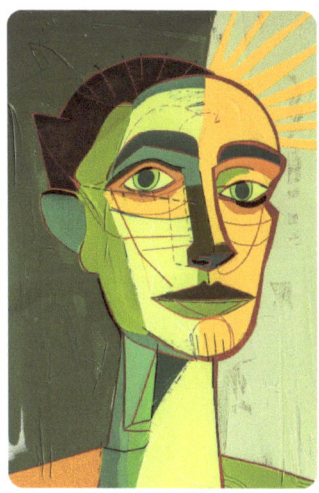

Female portrait, in the style of **Basquiat** --sref 1896223148

Nello stile di: **Van Gogh**

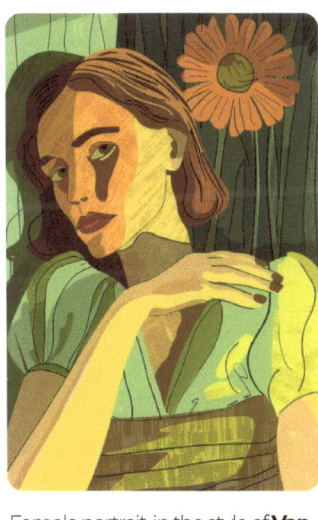

Female portrait, in the style of **Van Gogh** --sref 1896223148

Nello stile di: **Matisse**

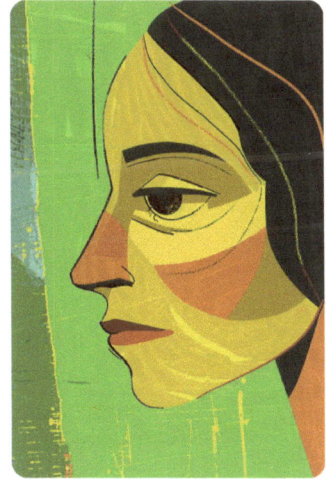

Female portrait, in the style of **Matisse** --sref 1896223148

Nello stile di: **Klimt**

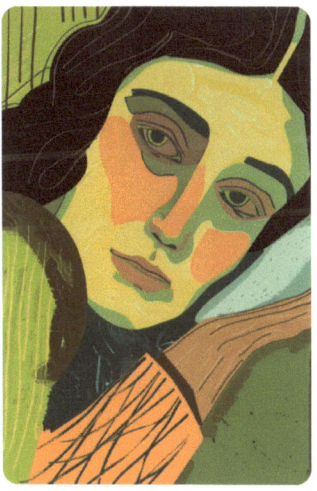

Female portrait, in the style of **Klimt** --sref 1896223148

But that's not all, you can also add other artists and mix more styles together. Try, for example, after "female portrait" to insert "in the style of **Matisse**, in the style of **Van Gogh**, in the style of **Klimt**, in the style of **Basquiat**, in the style of **Picasso**."

This is the result: an artistically interesting image, a work created through your personal research, a study in which artificial intelligence has become a valuable partner and not a substitute.

This is the result: an artistically interesting image, a work created through your personal research, a study in which artificial intelligence has become a valuable partner and not a substitute.

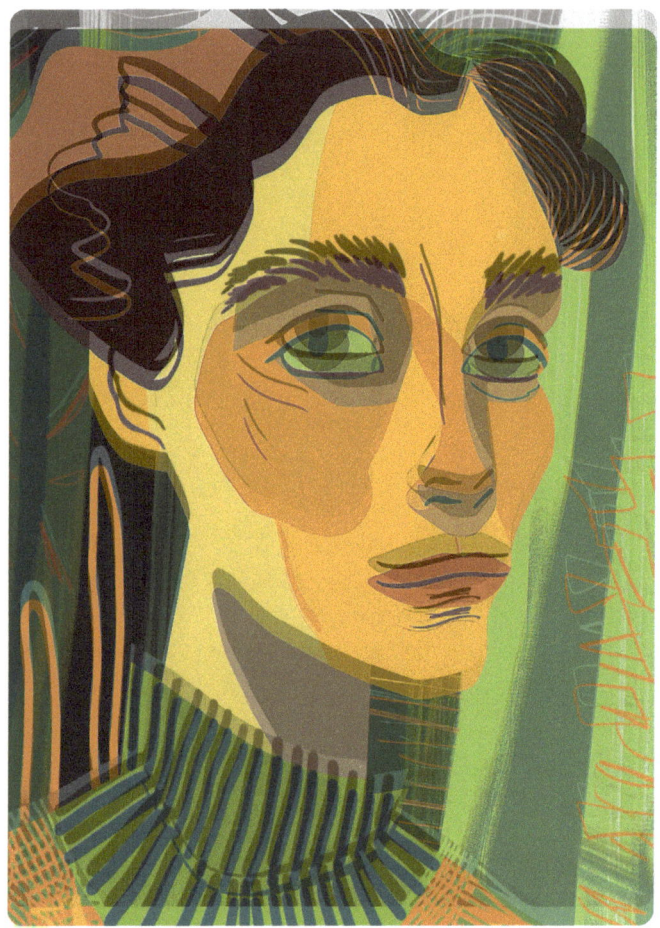

Female portrait, in the style of **Matisse**, in the style of **Van Gogh**, in the style of **Klimt**, in the style of **Basquiat**, in the style of **Picasso** --sref 1896223148 --ar 2:3

Female portrait, in the style of **Matisse**, in the style of **Van Gogh**, in the style of **Klimt**, in the style of **Basquiat**, in the style of **Picasso** --sref 1896223148 --ar 2:3

Finally, think about what I call the **magic phase** where you can mix **2** "--srefs" and get the "graphical sum" of the two values, an inimitable result that can become, if you wish, your personal artistic style.

Finally, think about what I call the **magic phase** where you can mix **2** "--srefs" and get the "graphical sum" of the two values, an inimitable result that can become, if you wish, your personal artistic style.

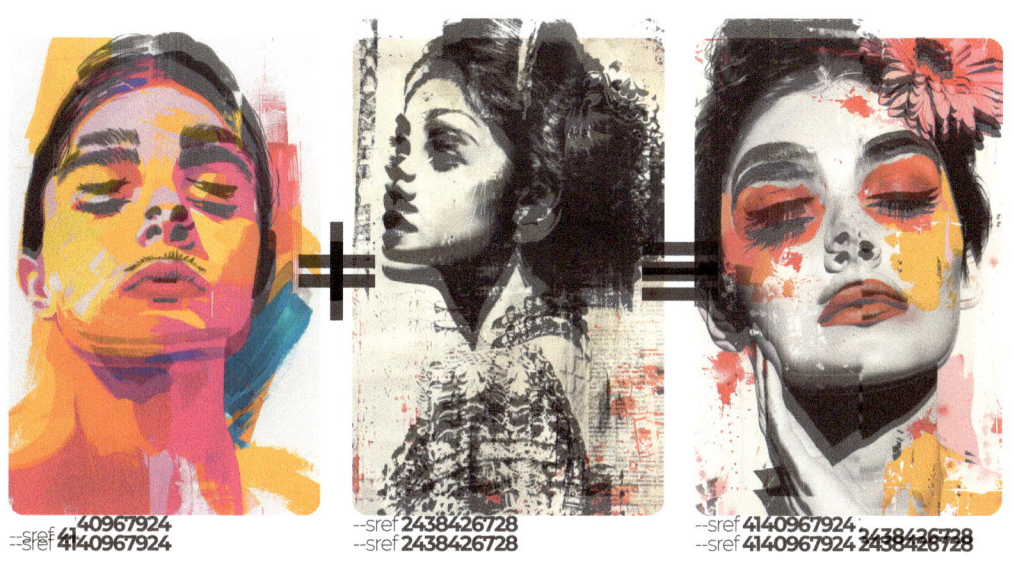

--sref **4140967924**
--sref **4140967924**

--sref **2438426728**
--sref **2438426728**

--sref **4140967924 2438426728**
--sref **4140967924 2438426728**

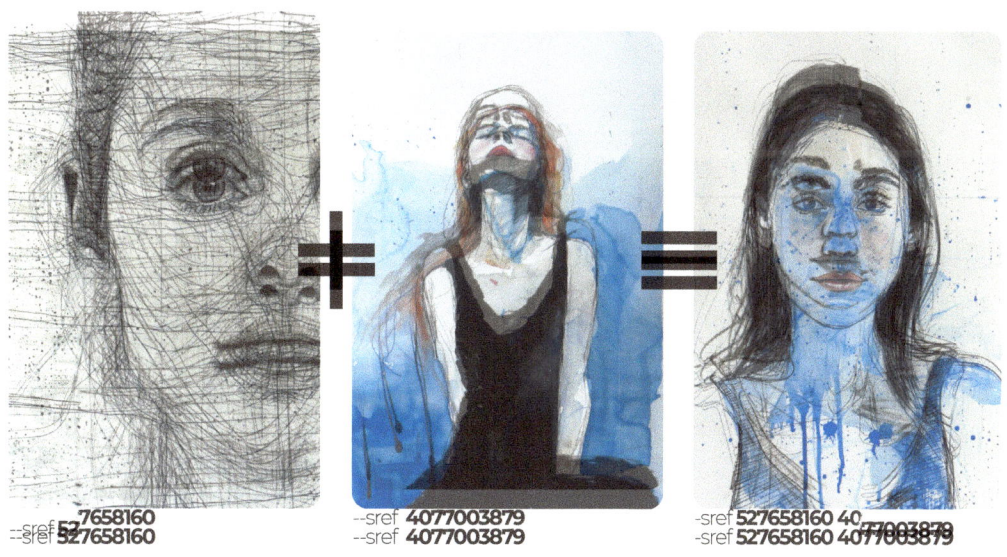

--sref **527658160**
--sref **527658160**

--sref **4077003879**
--sref **4077003879**

--sref **527658160 4077003879**
--sref **527658160 4077003879**

What if the end result was the sum of **3** "srefs"? Now it's just up to you, your desire to experiment and find the style that best represents you and that you feel belongs to you.

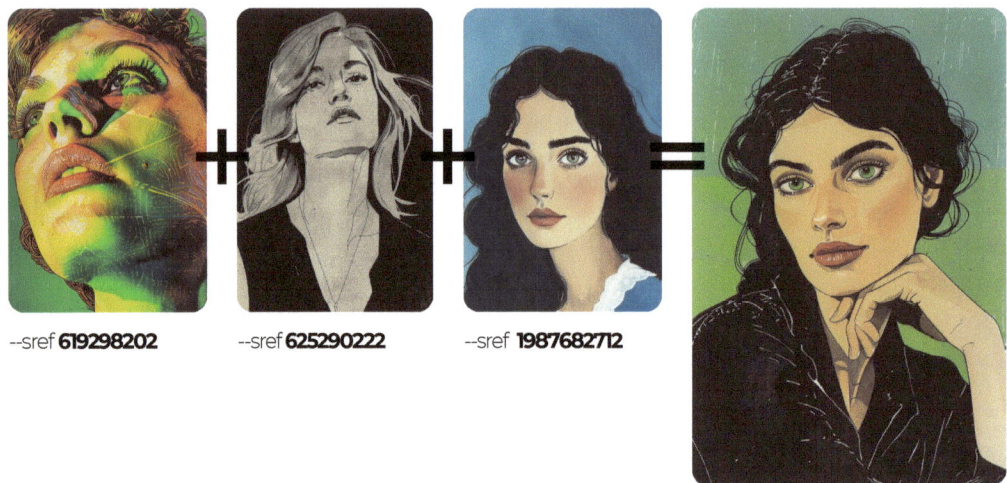

--sref **619298202**   --sref **625290222**   --sref **1987682712**

--sref **619298202 625290222 1987682712**

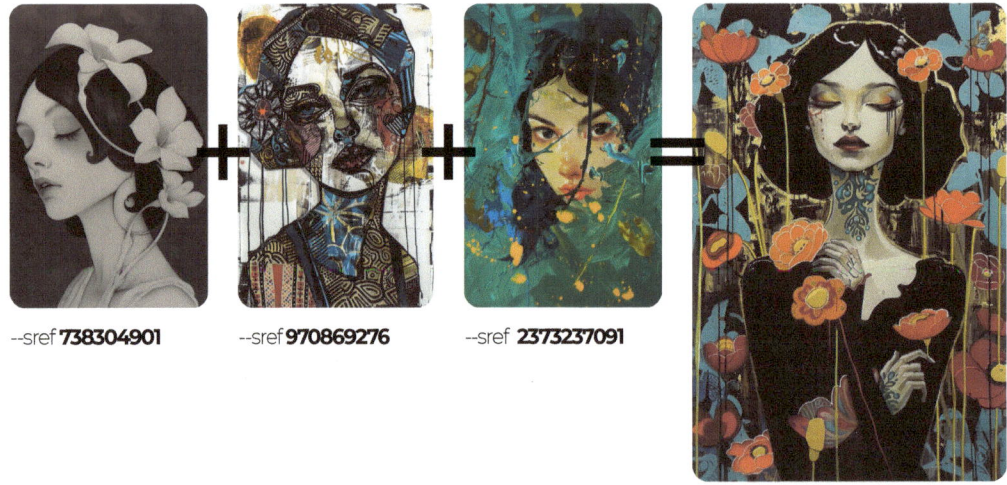

--sref **738304901**   --sref **970869276**   --sref **2373237091**

--sref **738304901 970869276 2373237091**

You can also try to add up **6 or more** and add the name of various artists. Your only limitation will be your imagination and imagination.

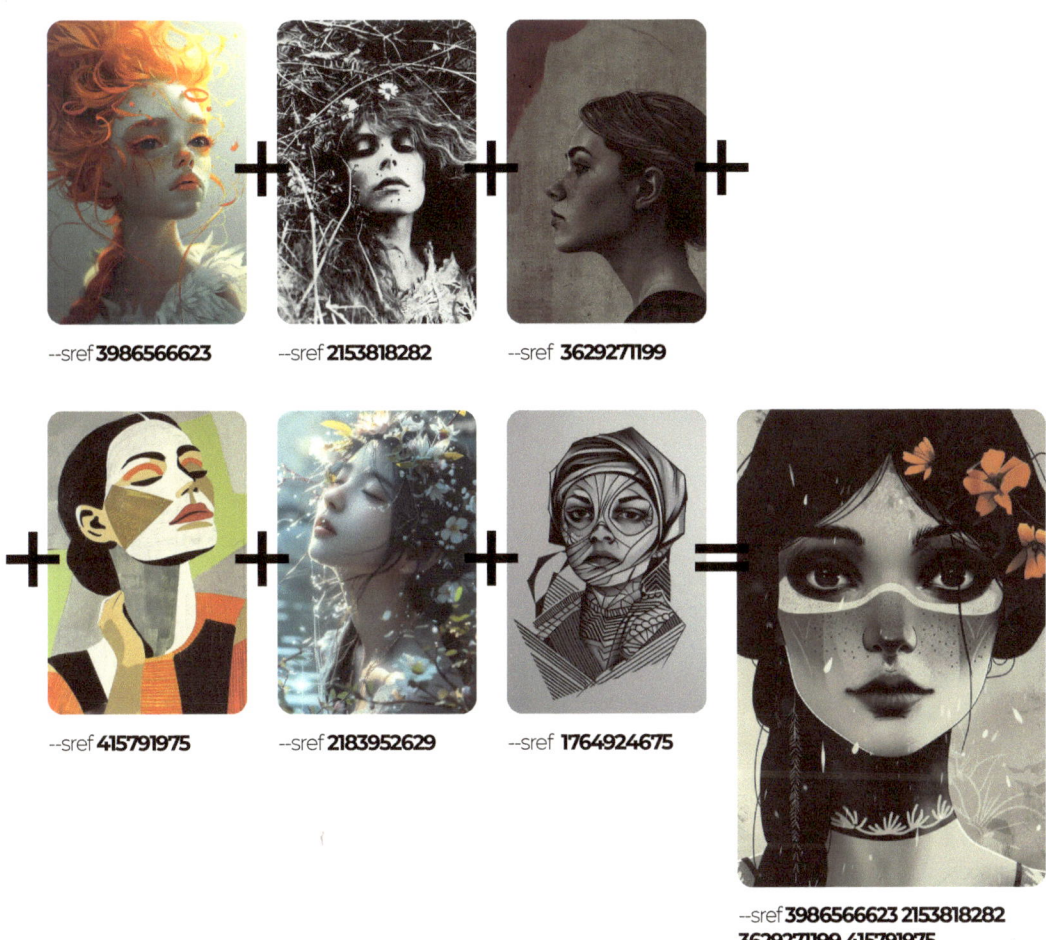

--sref **3986566623**

--sref **2153818282**

--sref **3629271199**

--sref **415791975**

--sref **2183952629**

--sref **1764924675**

--sref **3986566623 2153818282 3629271199 415791975 2183952629 1764924675**

I am sure that this brief journey into discovering MidJourney and the ability to use style codes has excited you as much as it has excited me.

The ability of this platform to transform ideas into extraordinary images is simply fascinating, and I hope you have experienced the same wonder and inspiration that I have felt on my journey.

Reflecting on what we have explored, I continue to question whether images generated by Artificial Intelligence can be considered art in the traditional sense of the term. It is not up to me to provide a definitive answer to this question, and perhaps there is no single answer.

However, I know that for each of the works I create, I have dedicated time and passion, trying to capture and represent my artistic vision. In this process, MidJourney has proven to be an incredibly powerful tool, capable of amplifying my creativity and taking my ideas to a visual level I could never have imagined.

But the truly surprising thing about MidJourney is that this platform enables what I call the **democratization of art**.

Now, anyone with an idea to develop can create fantastic images, even without knowing how to draw or mastering traditional artistic techniques.

This means that art becomes accessible to everyone, opening the doors to new forms of creative expression and allowing a broader audience to explore and share their artistic vision.

I am aware that for illustrators and those who have studied art for years, this technology might seem devastating.

The speed and efficiency with which MidJourney and other generative Artificial Intelligence platforms can create images might provoke concerns and resistance.

However, it is important to remember that no one is forcing traditional artists to use these tools. Every artist is free to choose the means they consider most suitable for expressing their creative vision.

Certainly, the path is now set, and we will not turn back. Technology advances unstoppably, and with it, the opportunities it offers.

What we can do is embrace these innovations as additional tools in our creative arsenal, capable of enriching and expanding our expressive possibilities.

Art has always benefited from innovation, evolving and adapting to technical and cultural changes. MJ represents a new and fascinating chapter in this ongoing evolution.

The democratization of art that this platform makes possible is not a threat but a celebration of human creativity in all its forms.

Now, a wider audience can explore and share their artistic vision, enriching the cultural landscape with a diversity of perspectives and styles..

MidJourney' is not just software; it is a revolution in the world of digital art.

It offers all of us the possibility to become creators, to experiment with styles and techniques, and to create works that reflect our uniqueness.

I hope this guide has provided you with the tools and inspiration to continue exploring and creating with MidJourney.

The creative adventure has just begun, and the possibilities are endless.
Happy creating!

Illustration of **Mirco Tangherlini**
tangherlini.it - ai-telier.it

Le immagini presenti in questo volume sono il frutto di collaborazioni innovative con diverse piattaforme di Intelligenza Artificiale all'avanguardia, dimostrando la straordinaria sinergia tra la creatività umana e la tecnologia IA.

Per gli appassionati che desiderano una connessione più personale se hai domande scrivimi su: mirco@tangherlini.it